Additional praise for
The Go Giver Influencer

"*The Go-Giver Influencer* is a simple story about two people struggling through a business negotiation, yet it is also a great deal more than that. It may just be the book that teaches us how to listen and talk to one another again."

—David Bach, author of *The Automatic Millionaire* and
Smart Women Finish Rich

"Filled with profoundly simple insights you can put into immediate action, *The Go-Giver Influencer* is a magical look at how you can transcend the win/lose mind-set to find a powerful third way. Thank you, Burg and Mann, for yet another Go-Giver book that helps us see the ordinary in extraordinary new ways. I will be sharing this book with everyone in my company!"

—Traci Fenton, founder and CEO of WorldBlu

"If you do nothing more than read and follow the lesson of chapter 7 in *The Go-Giver Influencer*, you will have given yourself a gift that can be life-changing. Trust me, it is the essential element to great leadership as well as a great life."

—Bob Chapman, CEO of Barry-Wehmiller and author of *Everybody Matters*

"What a beautiful book! *The Go-Giver Influencer* delivers a message the world needs today more than ever, a message of empathy and insight. This may be the most masterful Go-Giver book yet—and the most important."

—Nido R. Qubein, president of High Point University

"A must-read! *The Go-Giver Influencer* is a winner's strategy."

—Molly Fletcher, legendary sports agent; author of *A Winner's Guide to Negotiating*; and CEO of The Molly Fletcher Company

"Bob Burg and John David Mann have hit it out of the park again. *The Go-Giver Influencer* enriches and extends the seminal ideas of their previous works to creating harmony in an increasingly polarized world and win-win outcomes in your personal and professional lives. This book will sit beside Dale Carnegie's timeless *How to Win Friends and Influence People* on the short shelf of classic must-read success titles."

—Adam Robinson, cofounder of *The Princeton Review*

"Don't be fooled by this story's simplicity: Burg and Mann have given us a sophisticated blueprint for masterful negotiation. Not the tired old strong-arm tactics you've read before, but *genuine* negotiation, the kind that helps you reach your goals and makes the world a better place in the process."

—Brandon Webb, former Navy SEAL; CEO of Hurricane Media Group; and coauthor of *The Red Circle* and *Total Focus*

"Forget about influence as a process of simply getting your name, products, and services in front of as many people as you can. As the authors powerfully demonstrate, genuine influence is the fine art of building trust, creating win-win scenarios, and providing first-class value. I LOVE this book!"

—Libby Gill, author of *You Unstuck*; executive coach; former SVP at Universal Television; former VP at Sony Pictures Television and Turner Broadcasting

"The wisdom in *The Go Giver Influencer* sneaks up on you and, in the end, changes you. I loved the book and am the better for having read it."

—Dan Rockwell, publisher of the Leadership Freak blog

"A wonderful story that shows why being kind, considerate, and respectful is not only the right way to be, but also the most influential, persuasive, and successful way to be. In my real life, it's everything I believe in. On a reality TV show, of course, that would be a producer's worst nightmare—everyone would get along too well and be too happy!"

—Jacqueline Laurita, television personality of *The Real Housewives of New Jersey* and autism advocate

"*The Go-Giver Influencer* is like having a seasoned mentor or wise grandparent help improve the way you negotiate, influence, and persuade, and—most important—stop being a roadblock to your own success. You'll want to buy copies for all your valued colleagues!"

—Carol Roth, founder of the Future File® legacy planning system; television host; and author of *The Entrepreneur Equation*

"A masterpiece—profound and vital. Thank you, Bob and John, for writing the perfect book at the perfect time with the most perfect message."

—Lolly Daskal, author of *The Leadership Gap*

"*The Go-Give Influencer* is a beautiful story that redefines and reframes our notion of leadership, influence, and the legacy we want to leave. A true gift for all who want to make an impact."

—Angela Maiers, author of *Genius Matters* and founder of Choose2Matter

"In *The Go-Giver Influencer*, Bob Burg and John David Mann provide incredibly wise counsel on how to communicate more successfully and more effectively. This entertaining parable reveals step-by-step how you can add value to every conversation you have, while achieving the greatest results for everyone involved."

—Sharon Lechter, author of *Think and Grow Rich for Women*; coauthor of *Outwitting the Devil* and *Rich Dad, Poor Dad*

"Compelling reading for anyone who seeks to influence without manipulation and negotiate with integrity. *The Go-Giver Influencer* is as much a philosophy for living as it is for conducting business with honor and ethics. It will make you rethink everything you've learned about negotiation and influence, and help you to be better at both."

—Gary Pittard, author of *Why Winners Win* and CEO of
Pittard Real Estate Training

"Who do you want to be in the world? *The Go-Giver Influencer* shows us the path forward to become wiser, smarter, and more humane leaders at a time when that's needed more than ever."

—Dorie Clark, author of *Entrepreneurial You* and adjunct professor at
Duke University's Fuqua School of Business

"A brilliant book that will help you influence and impact with the best."

—Robin Sharma, author of *The Leader Who Had No Title* and
The Monk Who Sold His Ferrari

"If we are paying attention, mentors will show up (with perfect timing). Sometimes they appear as people helping us simplify what feels complicated . . . 'untying the knots.' Sometimes these mentors are wrapped in a powerful story; they 'mentor the multitudes.' Bob Burg and John David Mann, you've done it again! Reading this book is like unwrapping a lovely gift."

—Dondi Scumaci, author of *Designed for Success* and *Career Moves*

"Leaders looking to improve their negotiation and communication skills will find very helpful insights in *The Go-Giver Influencer*."

—Douglas R. Conant, founder and CEO, ConantLeadership; chairman,
Kellogg Executive Leadership Institute at Northwestern University; former
CEO, Campbell Soup Company; former chairman, Avon Products

The Go-Giver Influencer

The Go-Giver Influencer

A Little Story About a
Most Persuasive Idea

Bob Burg *and* John David Mann

Bestselling authors of *The Go-Giver*

PORTFOLIO / PENGUIN

Portfolio/Penguin
An imprint of Penguin Random House LLC
375 Hudson Street
New York, New York 10014

Most Portfolio books are available at a discount when purchased in quantity for
sales promotions or corporate use. Special editions, which include personalized
covers, excerpts, and corporate imprints, can be created when purchased in large
quantities. For more information, please call (212) 572-2232 or e-mail
specialmarkets@penguinrandomhouse.com. Your local bookstore can also assist
with discounted bulk purchases using the Penguin Random House corporate
Business-to-Business program. For assistance in locating a participating retailer,
e-mail B2B@penguinrandomhouse.com.

ISBN: 9781591846376 (hardcover)
ISBN: 9780525533702 (e-book)

Printed in the United States of America
1   3   5   7   9   10   8   6   4   2

Book design by George Towne

To Mike and Myrna Burg,
Alfred and Carolyn Mann,
and Ana Gabriel Mann,
whose influence on us has shaped
everything in our lives

and to the four-legged creatures of the world—those
angels clothed in fur—who make life richer and sweeter
for humans everywhere.

CONTENTS

Introduction

It's hard to believe it's been a full decade since the first few copies of *The Go-Giver* stepped onto the bookshelves to state their message and see if the world was interested in reading about Pindar's Paradox—that *the more you give, the more you have.*

Turned out, the world was.

Most books enjoy an initial surge of sales and interest and then taper off to a relatively quiet life in the wings—the *backlist*, as publishers call it. With *The Go-Giver*, things went rather in the opposite direction: with each succeeding year, rather than diminishing, interest seemed to keep growing. And growing.

Something about the book seemed to touch a chord, often in the most unexpected places. Originally positioned as a *business* book, our "little story about a powerful business idea" began showing up in book clubs, community groups, sermons, and high school classrooms, as well as in boardrooms and sales-and-service trainings. CEOs and thought leaders were quoting it. It started becoming not simply popular, but *influential.*

In 2015, our publisher brought out a new expanded edition of the book, with a foreword and introduction, a Discussion Guide for readers' groups, additional commentary—and a curious feature on the back jacket that to us was both fascinating and significant: the handful of endorsements there were bracketed by a pair of quotes from Arianna Huffington and Glenn Beck. Not two people whose views you'd typically expect to find on the same page (whether metaphorically or, as in this case, literally).

Which brings us to the reason for the book you're now holding in your hands and the true meaning and value of *influence*.

The idea of influence has been at the center of all three Go-Giver books to date.

In *The Go-Giver*, Sam Rosen, the beaming white-haired insurance man, explains to Joe that grasping the true nature of influence became the key to his success—and that people typically get it backward:

> "If you asked most people what creates influence, what would they say?"
>
> Joe's answer came without hesitation. "Money. Position. Maybe a history of outstanding accomplishments."
>
> Sam nodded, grinning. "Ha! You're right, that's *exactly* what they'd say—and they'd have it exactly backwards! Those things don't *create* influence—influence creates *them*."

He also defined what he called the Law of Influence:

"Your influence is determined by how abundantly you place other people's interests first."

In *Go-Givers Sell More*, the third of its five parts—the keystone at the center of the book's arch—expounded and expanded on that law and how it works in everyday real-life operation.

In *The Go-Giver Leader*, in a chapter entitled "The Substance of Influence," Aunt Elle (that book's mentor figure) offers up this definition of influence:

"Well," she said, hitching forward eagerly in her seat, "the word *influence* means *an unseen flow of power*. It was first used in the Middle Ages, believe it or not, as an astrological term, from an Old French word meaning *a streaming ethereal power from the stars acting upon our character or destiny*. Imagine that!

"By the fifteenth century, the word was being used to mean *an exercise of personal power by human beings*. You could say, it describes how we exert gravitational force on each other. Like stars."

We thought Sam, Aunt Elle, and the rest had pretty well summed it up. But the world moves on, and its needs change and evolve. If Pindar and his friends were here today, we wondered, participating in the world of 2018, what would they say? What would they want to write about? Influence, we thought, for sure—but perhaps more specifically about the role influence plays in the capacity for empathy and civil discourse.

At its heart, *The Go-Giver Influencer* is a story about what it takes to bridge differences, to settle disputes and defang conflicts, to find common ground where there appear to be only irreconcilably polarized positions. (And, yes, even to negotiate business dealings.) It is also about what it takes to be the kind of person whom others come to trust, a person to whom others look for sound guidance, clear judgment, and, in times of challenge, evenhanded wisdom.

A person, in other words, of genuine influence.

In recent years the term "influencer" has come into widespread usage, a development we greatly appreciate. The more society explores the nature and significance of positive influence, the better off our world becomes. We thought Pindar's friends would have something uniquely Pindarian to say about that—and we hope that, once you've arrived at the final toast that closes this story, you'll agree.

Bob Burg and John David Mann
January 2018

1: Jackson

Jackson Hill looked like a man waiting to see the executioner.

"Are you sure you won't have some coffee?" The young woman at the reception desk had already offered him coffee, a soft drink, and water, in that order.

"I'm good. Thanks, though." He liked her energy. The nameplate on her desk said MIRABEL. *Perfect*, thought Jackson. *That's exactly what I need today. A* MIRACLE.

He glanced at the wall clock. Ten after. Eleven, now. It had taken three weeks just to get this appointment. Three weeks he couldn't afford to wait. And now the appointed hour had come . . . and here he was, still waiting. He suppressed the impulse to look at the clock again. After three weeks of waiting, another ten minutes—no, eleven—shouldn't matter, right?

"Yes . . ." Mirabel was speaking into her headset now. "Okay. I'll send him in." She smiled at Jackson and said, "Ms. Waters can see you now. It's straight down the hall, on the right."

Finally.

As Jackson walked past her desk, Mirabel leaned forward a little and spoke in a stage whisper. "You're going to *love* Ms. Waters. She's really nice."

Jackson hoped that was true.

As he took his seat, Jackson noticed a photo on Ms. Waters's desk of a young girl (twelve, maybe?) curled around a beautiful Russian Blue cat, looking at the camera with big solemn eyes that said, *This is MY cat. Nobody messes with MY cat.* The elegant Blue stared at the camera, too, with haunting green eyes that said, *This is MY human. Nobody messes with MY human.*

Jackson smiled. Maybe this meeting would go well after all.

"So," the woman said, still looking down at the papers on her desk. "Mr. Hall."

"Hill," said Jackson, already feeling defensive.

She looked up. "Sorry?"

"It's Hill. Jackson Hill."

"Of course. Mr. Hill. Jackson. So," she sat back in her chair to give him her full attention. "Tell me about your business."

Showtime.

"Sure. So, we started with our first line of dry dog food, five years ago. That was just for dogs. All different sizes and ages. And then within six months, we added a cat line . . . ," and he went on, just as he'd rehearsed it, chronicling how over the past five years he'd built his fledgling business into a respected brand.

Of course, when he used the words "we started" and "we

added," he was really talking about just himself, Jackson, working solo in his cramped little kitchen, late into the nights and over long weekends, experimenting, crafting, adjusting. *Only the purest,* as his company motto went, *only the freshest, only the best.* Jackson had in every sense built his business from his kitchen table.

"Quite the entrepreneur," said Ms. Waters.

He shifted in his seat, unsure exactly how to respond to that.

Jackson had never intended to be a business owner. All he wanted was to see animals have the best food to eat. He'd just had to become an entrepreneur in order to do it. Six years ago he was working a sales job for an electronics outlet (and hating it), cooking for himself, Walt, and Solomon. When he shared his natural dog food concoctions with a few friends who also lived with dogs, word got out. By the time he let go of his sales job to focus full time on his pet food line, he had more than a hundred customers—and that widely respected brand.

All of which could come crashing down exactly one week from today if he didn't get this contract.

No, not *could.* All of which *would* come crashing down.

"So, you distribute to, what, now"—she was glancing down again, running her finger down the sheet at the top of her little stack of papers—"two states?"

"Three," he said. "Almost four," he added, and immediately regretted it. Almost four? What, like holding four fingers up high and proudly saying, "These many!" *You're in business now, Jackie,* as Walt would say. *You gotta act like it.*

"Three," said Ms. Waters, nodding to her papers. "Almost

four." She looked up and leveled her gaze directly at Jackson. "So tell me: Why do we want to carry you?"

Jackson winced. He knew she meant to say, "carry *your products*," right? But intentionally or not, she'd certainly nailed it, hadn't she. If—*if*—they gave him this contract, they would indeed be carrying *him*.

He took a breath.

"It's simple, really. I love animals. Adore them. Big, small, two-day-old kittens, old hounds on their last legs, doesn't matter what shape or size or breed or temperament, to me they are all, every one of them, the noblest, sweetest, kindest, most . . . well, most authentic creatures. I look at an animal like"—he almost said, *Like your daughter's cat*, but would that be getting too personal?—"well, like any cat, any dog, and I think they were put here as emissaries of how we ought to be. Emissaries of heaven on earth."

Ms. Waters smiled thinly. "Hence, the name."

Jackson nodded. "Exactly. That's how I see them."

She looked down at the papers again. " 'Angels Clothed in Fur.' " And up again at Jackson. "A somewhat unconventional name for a business."

"We're a somewhat unconventional business," he said, feeling defensive again. "Anyway, as I said, it's simple. I want to reach more animals with the best the earth has to offer. Only the purest and freshest. That slogan—I really mean it. And if I can put my product in your stores, well, you can reach a lot more creatures than I can on my own."

Understatement of the week. Smith & Banks Pet Supply, the

chain Ms. Waters represented, had stores in every state coast to coast. A massive footprint. Or should he say, pawprint.

Ms. Waters glanced at her papers again, then back at Jackson and smiled once more, that thin smile that didn't seem to give much away.

"Well, I've looked through the materials you sent, and I have to say it's impressive. We like it, and we like you. We are definitely interested in the possibilities."

Jackson's heart leapt. He nearly leapt, too, right out of his chair. *Impressive—we like it, and we like you.* Wow!

Then his head caught up. Hang on, did she just say, "definitely . . . *possibilities*"? Wasn't that sort of like saying, "For sure . . . maybe"?

"We think Angels Clothed in Fur could sit very comfortably on our shelves," Ms. Waters was saying. "Just two points. You'd need to supply us on a national basis, of course. And we would want it to be an exclusive arrangement."

Jackson's heart stopped.

National?

Exclusive?

National distribution—that would mean he'd either have to ship his products clear across the country, which would be impossible, because part of his whole thing was their freshness and emphasis on locally grown ingredients . . . or he'd have to set up not one or two but at least a *dozen* separate production sites. Which would take an enormous investment. Which was completely out of the question.

And, *exclusive*? Pull out of all his existing clients' stores?

Turn his back on all those relationships? It hurt even to think about it.

"Okay," he said, his heart racing, desperately hoping that she couldn't see how rattled he was. "See, I was hoping to start out going into stores in four states, maybe five. I mean, that's what we're geared for at the moment."

"I understand," she said. "But you understand, we're a national chain. Providing *only the purest, only the best* in these five states over here, but not in those five states over there . . . well, would that be fair to our customers?"

Jackson felt his face flush. *Would that be a rhetorical question?* he wanted to say, but he bit it back. Instead he just sighed. (Silently—he hoped.) "No, of course, I see your point. But I don't see how . . ."

He stopped. How did he plan to finish that sentence?

The silence in the room felt positively chilly.

He had to say *something*, but he didn't dare explain his actual situation.

Revenue from those early clients had allowed him to take over an old out-of-business diner. With his own industrial kitchen, he had built out his pet food line and extended his sales to stores across the state. To extend that reach farther to cover three states—well, *parts* of three states—he'd had to set up a whole new separate production facility in the next state over so he could keep to his standards of freshness and local supply.

But setting up and running a new plant from scratch was a lot harder than he expected. The financing he'd gotten to do it was drowning him. The bank had been patient for a year, but now he had to bring his account current, or they would call the loan and shut down his operation. A week from today. There was no way under the sun he could come up with the cash—but if he could show up with a large purchase order from a major national company, he was betting, that would halt the process and keep his doors open. A contract with Ms. Waters's company, in other words, might just save him from going under.

And at that thought, an idea slipped into his mind, so quietly that it took him a moment to realize it was sitting there waiting for him.

"I understand what you're saying," he said. "That makes sense. I see that. Of course, to scale up on that level, I'd need some assistance."

For the first time since their meeting had begun, Ms. Waters looked ever so slightly taken off balance. "Assistance?"

"Well," said Jackson, "the entire continental United States, that's a good deal of territory. Our whole thing is *fresh and local*. That's more or less the heart of the brand. The brand you'd be featuring on your shelves. We'd need to put in place a network of kitchens—production centers. We have several now." (He had two, barely.) "To supply nationwide, we'd need to set up, oh, a dozen more around the country, I'd expect. A dozen at least. That'd take a little financing."

He tried to say this all in an entirely neutral, casual tone. Oh, sure, a dozen plants across the country. What he was planning to do anyway. *A little financing?* Just saying the words nearly gave him a heart attack.

"I don't mean you'd provide actual *funding*," he added.

"That would have to come from my own sources, obviously. But I've never gone into anything on this scale before. The only way it would work, I expect, would be with someone big, someone like Smith and Banks, underwriting it. Guaranteeing the loan, I mean."

Ms. Waters regarded him with an appraising look.

"Right. Well, I can certainly run that past the Corner Office, see what they say. But to be honest, Mr. Hill, I can't promise they'll be friendly about the idea."

Another chilly silence.

"Also, you said, an exclusive?"

She raised her eyebrows, as if to say, *Yes?*

"That's . . . that's a tall order. Right now I supply a lot of stores in our area."

She said nothing. *And?*

"A lot of these small stores, these aren't just clients, they're friends. People I've known for years." And without whom his business would never have gotten off the ground, he could have added.

"Of course," she said. "You've got an existing pipeline. Agreements and contracts. We assumed there'd be a transition period. Time for you to fulfill your current obligations and gracefully withdraw from future commitments, work up new marketing collateral for our stores, and so forth. Say, three months?"

Jackson nodded numbly. *Marketing collateral.* He hadn't thought about that.

Unexpectedly, Ms. Waters's voice softened. "I know, it's a lot."

She was silent again for a moment—though this time some-how the silence did not feel so chilly.

"Tell you what, Mr. Hill," she said after another moment. "Why don't you go back and talk with your people, see what you might be able to work out. And I'll go speak with the Corner Office here about that underwriting idea. And then we'll meet again, okay? Say, next Friday, a week from today?"

A week from today. Exactly the words the bank officer had spoken to him that morning—only without the question mark.

He stood up, reached over her desk, and shook her hand.

"A week," he said. "Thank you."

You've got this, Jackson, he told himself as he slipped past Mirabel's desk with a nod and a mouthed *Thank you!* (she was on the phone) and showed himself out the door. *You are a successful businessman. You are going to close this deal.* But it didn't feel like he was going to close this deal. And he didn't feel like a successful businessman.

He felt like a man who had just been to see the executioner.

2: Gillian

Gillian stared out her office window, trying to see her future.

Ten long years she'd been here. She was smart, and she worked hard, but it had been a struggle just to get where she was. A buyer. "Ms. Gray Flannel Suit," Katie would say, poking fun at her. "Ms. Mid-Level Executive." Well, that's what she was, and proud of it. Her company did a lot of good, and she was part of that.

But she was aiming higher. She wanted that Corner Office.

Everyone in the company knew that the senior VP of Distribution was about to retire. (It was the company's best-kept secret, ha-ha.) Gillian wanted that spot. If she got it, maybe someday she might even run the company. Hey, why not?

If she got it, more to the point, she would command a salary that would let her put Bo in that school she wanted, and save for her college. And buy her a horse. And give her the world. Because the kid deserved it.

Gillian felt her heart lurch.

She turned back to her desk and pushed the TALK button

on the office intercom. "Mirabel?" she said. "Could you see about getting me an appointment with the Corner Office?"

"Sure, Ms. Waters," the voice said back. "For when?"

"As soon as he can see me," she said. "Monday, hopefully."

"We'll give it our best shot, Ms. Waters."

"You're the best, Mirabel," said Gillian, and she clicked off.

Only the purest, only the freshest, only the best.

When she'd said she was impressed with Jackson Hill's company, she wasn't kidding. His products were good—really good. She'd wanted to meet with him right away when he first contacted their office, but she'd needed a few weeks to research his company and his products. She bought samples, talked with customers, even went out and talked with store owners, including some of his oldest clients. The more she dug, the better it all looked.

No doubt to him she appeared fairly ignorant of his company—but that was just strategy. Better to keep it opaque. *Never show your cards,* as Craig would say. (Although look how *that* had turned out.)

She didn't feel great about that. But she didn't just want Jackson's line. She *needed* it. Not only would it be a great account to win. It was an account that could make her career.

If she could bring Jackson's unique line in-house, it would be a huge feather in her cap—which would put her within spitting distance of that promotion to senior VP of Distribution. Competition for that position would be fierce, no question about it. Gillian was no good at office politics, but she knew this much for certain: if she could land the Jackson Hill account, she would have a shot at it.

She turned in her chair and looked outside again, now at the fading light. She didn't want to go home, not just yet. She hated going home when the place was empty.

She thought back to their conversation that morning, when she'd dropped Bo off at school, and smiled.

"Looking forward to seeing your dad this weekend?" she'd said.

Bo squirmed in the car seat. "I guess. He's always busy."

That was Craig, all right. Always busy. "Busy, how?" she countered.

Bo gave a theatrical sigh. "On his laptop, and on the phone." Big gestures with both hands. "And stuff."

Gillian smiled. "*I'm* always busy, too, Bo-bird."

"That's different."

"Different, how?"

"Mom." Her daughter gave her a look that said, *Do I really have to explain this?* "Even when you're busy, you're still *here*. You're never *busy* busy."

Gillian felt her heart lurch again, like it did a thousand times a day.

No, not home, not yet. She took a big breath. She was done here for the day. So, if not home, then where? Ha. As if she had to ask.

Ten minutes in and she had already worked up a serious sweat—but she was just getting started. She sat up, reached down and added five more pounds to the weight machine, then lay back down on the bench and resumed her overhead chest extensions. Total weight: thirty pounds.

Push. Slow release. Push. Slow release. Push . . .

Gillian was ambitious, it was true. But it was more than that. And yes, she wanted a salary that would allow her to take the best care of her daughter, whom she loved with the fierceness of a mother tiger. But if she were honest with herself, it was more than that, too. She wanted to feel her own efforts having an impact, a real impact. That was why she'd joined this company in the first place, not just to keep a roof over their heads but because she wanted to make a *difference*.

She sat up and added more weight, then lay back down and kept going.

Forty pounds.

She didn't understand Jackson Hill's reluctance. She was offering him something even bigger than what he was asking for. Why wasn't he jumping at it? He seemed strangely uneasy and uncooperative. She could not figure the guy out. Did he want this contract or not?

She'd been positive they would end that meeting with at least an agreement in principle, details to be worked out in the days ahead. But he seemed to back up from every term and condition she put on the table.

And that request, to underwrite his "kitchens," she had not seen that coming. He had to know that was a huge ask. Big enough that she would now have to go get buy-in from the senior VP himself. The very guy whose position she hoped to land.

She sat up and added more weight.

Fifty pounds. Push, slow release . . .

She thought about the week ahead. Sunday afternoon she'd get Bo back. Sunday evening they would have a blast together.

And then Monday.

She didn't know which was going to be the bigger challenge: getting the Corner Office to agree to put its credit behind the financing for Jackson's string of "kitchens" or keeping Jackson himself from bolting at the first loud noise, like a skittish colt. When she'd said *national* and *exclusive*, she thought she was going to have to hit the intercom and ask Mirabel to bring a defibrillator.

Sixty pounds.

Actually, now that she thought about it, that was easy, no contest: *both* challenges were impossible. But she had to walk out of that meeting next Friday with a signed contract in her hand. *Had* to.

She groaned out loud.

"Were you bad?"

Gillian paused in her reps and looked up into the face looking down at hers. Even upside down, Katie's brightly freckled face made her want to laugh. "What?"

"Were you very bad? I think you've been very bad. 'Cause you sure are punishing yourself."

Gillian sighed and sat up.

Katie was not only her dedicated trainer but also her best friend. She wasn't sure which she really came here for, the workouts or the "talkouts."

That one was easy, too: both.

"I'm trying to land this account," said Gillian, "the one I told you about?"

Katie nodded as she grabbed Gillian's arm and tugged her over toward another machine.

"I don't know what the guy's story is, but it feels like I'm pulling up a tree stump with a piece of thread. If I pull too hard, the thread'll break—but if I don't pull at all, he'll just sit there."

"Like a stump," volunteered Katie.

"Exactly. Thank you."

"Sit."

Katie had Gillian lie down on the bench, then set the weights and gave her leg a *Let's go!* whack. Gillian obediently started doing her leg lifts. Forty pounds.

"I really need this, Katie. It's the only way I'm going to have a crack at that Corner Office—the only way I'm ever going to get Bo into that school—"

"Etcetera." Katie nodded. "I know, sweetie. I know."

Gillian had gone through another twenty reps before it dawned on her that Katie was standing there, just watching her. She dropped her feet down onto the floor, took a big breath, and looked at her friend. "What."

"Maybe you should go see the coach," said Katie.

Gillian stood up and put her hands on Katie's shoulders, looking her in the face. "Katie. You're not only my best friend and the biggest pain in the neck I know, you're also my trainer. *My* trainer. I don't need to work with another coach."

"Not *a* coach," said Katie. "*The* Coach."

Gillian sat back down on the bench. "*What* coach?" she said, as she resumed her leg lifts.

"This guy," said Katie. "I think he used to be a football coach or something, like high school. I don't know if he was ever pro or not. But now he's some kind of high-level executive coach, works with CEOs and people in high-stress positions, things like that."

"Help me," said Gillian. "And this miracle-working motivational guru's name is . . . ?"

Katie pursed her lips in thought. "I don't think . . ." She shrugged. "No, I don't think I ever heard it mentioned. My client, the one who's worked with him? She always just calls him 'the Coach.' Says he teaches this thing he calls his Winning Strategy. Here," Katie fished out her phone as she talked, "I'll text you his number."

Gillian made a face. "Aha. His Winning Strategy. Fantastic. Probably an ax murderer who lures women like me to their doom with sweet promises of corporate jets and their face on magazine covers."

Katie swatted her on the thigh. "You're terrible!"

Gillian nodded. "Yes. I am. Now, back to my punishment."

She reached forward, adjusted the weights, sat back, grabbed the handles, and continued her reps.

Fifty pounds . . .

Ninety minutes later, Gillian stepped into her front vestibule, closed the door, and heard it go *click!* She stood, motionless. When Bo was away and the house was empty like this, the silence was so thick it felt like it had a weight, a density all its own. Like a spell cast over a dark forest while a princess slept for a century.

She felt something brush against her leg.

She looked down and smiled at Cleo silently twining her tail around Gillian's leg. She mimed blowing a kiss at Cleo, without making a sound. For some reason, the silence felt to her as if it should not be broken, not yet. Like an enchantment. Like if she broke the spell, her daughter would never be returned to her but would sleep in the dark forest forever.

She shook her head abruptly. "The things a mother thinks," she said aloud.

Cleo looked up at her and silently agreed.

Gillian slipped off her shoes and padded to the kitchen to make herself a cup of hot tea.

A high school football coach. Seriously? His "Winning Strategy"?

Give me a break.

While waiting for her tea to cool enough for a sip, Gillian Waters sat on a kitchen stool, staring out the window, trying to see her future.

After a few minutes, she reached into a pocket and pulled out her phone.

3: The Dog Park

When Jackson arrived home, his place was the opposite of empty.

The commotion began when he was still ten feet from the entrance; by the time his hand was on the doorknob, it had escalated to a five-alarm ruckus. He opened the door and was immediately swallowed in an onslaught of crushing weight, hot breath, and a tongue the size of a hand towel.

"Whoa, buddy!" Jackson collapsed under the mass of dog, laughing and protesting and giving up all at the same time. When Solomon was present, all available space was taken up, no matter how big the space was. His hundred and fifty pounds could fill a small couch. His personality could fill an auditorium. When Solomon greeted you, you *stayed* greeted.

"I love you, too, buddy."

By way of agreement, Solomon took two steps back and shook off.

Solomon shaking himself always created a burst of sound, all clanging collar and tags and rapid-fire back-and-forth whapping of those big ears—it sounded to Jackson like a helicopter coming in for a landing at close range. What did they call the president's helicopter? Marine One. A new nickname. *Meet my dog, Marine One.* Whenever Sol shook off, Jackson would now imagine the first few bars of "Hail to the Chief."

"Hey, buddy"—Solomon now came to a complete stop, eyes and ears glued on Jackson to catch his next words— "wanna hit the trail?"

Now *there* was a rhetorical question. Before Jackson had finished the word *trail*, Solomon was steamrolling down the front hall, and a moment later here he was, back again, leash in his mouth.

"Taking Sol to the park!" Jackson called out as he hooked leash to collar.

From somewhere in the apartment's interior a reply drifted back. "*Yup.*" Man of few words, was Walter Hill. Sometimes, anyway.

"Back soon!" he added, and left without expecting an answer.

Jackson loved taking Solomon out for walks. Though to be fair, it would be more accurate to say it was Solomon who took Jackson.

It didn't take long to catch up with Lily and Keith. Lily, Keith's pit bull, was a rescue dog; she was also one of Solomon's favorite dog-park dates.

This was Jackson's favorite part of the whole Solomon-walking experience. He loved watching the dogs meet up, the enthusiasm, the sheer unbridled joy of it. It was one of the biggest reasons he so loved being around dogs: they always reminded him to appreciate the miracle of simply being alive, sniffing the air, feeling the breeze, the unabashed exuberance of being able to rocket (or even just to *walk*, for heaven's sake; just look at poor Keith) through space on a pair of legs. Or two pairs. The things human beings seemed to take for granted, but dogs never did.

Keith was a retired fireman, although Jackson thought "retired" probably was not really the right term for someone still in his fifties. Some years back he'd been in a bad accident on the job, and was now living on disability. His right leg didn't function that well and never would, but he worked it every day, taking it out for long walks with Lily. (Whose legs worked just fine.)

For the hundredth time, Jackson marveled that he and Keith were friends. They were from entirely different generations, different neighborhoods, different life experiences. There was very little they agreed on, and absolutely nothing they had in common.

The two men stood side by side, watching the spectacle of Solomon and Lily turning in circles around each other and sniffing each other all over.

Okay *one* thing in common.

The dogs now took off across the park, and the two men started ambling along the path while the dogs careened back and forth, circling and chasing each other madly, taking turns as lion and gazelle, playing catch-and-growl-and-release, grinning and throwing off strings of drool and having the kind of full-out delighted playtime that only dogs and children seem to speak as their native tongue.

The two men chuckled.

"Damnedest thing, isn't it?" said Keith. "They see each other, and it's the world's greatest reunion. Like they've been apart for ten years. The World War II sailor kissing the nurse in Times Square."

"I know," said Jackson as they walked. "I love it."

For some odd reason, watching those dogs having the time of their lives brought him back to those miserably tense minutes in Ms. Waters's office. Not a whole lot of enthusiasm and unbridled joy in *that* meeting, that was for sure. All at once Jackson felt glum. "Animals, I understand," he added. "It's people I have a hard time getting."

"Huh." Keith gave a brief sideways glance. "Hard day at the office, dear?"

That got a laugh out of Jackson. No matter how lousy he felt, Keith could always get him laughing. "You could say."

He laid out the situation for Keith in broad strokes. "So," he concluded, "we meet again next Friday. And if I don't walk out of that meeting with a contract in my hand, I'm out of business. It's over."

"Huh," said Keith again. He picked up some gravelly dirt, rubbed it between his hands, then tossed it down again. Jackson never knew why he did that, but it seemed to help him think.

"Jackson, you are dog's best friend, and a stellar human being at that. But when it comes to understanding the subtleties of business, you are a few pups short of a litter."

Jackson sighed.

"You need to learn some tricks of the trade, my friend."

"And which trade would that be, Keith?"

Keith gave Jackson his signature *What are you, an idiot?* look. "Business, man. You have to close your deal, right? You need to learn how to negotiate. Maneuver. *Tricks and tactics*, man, *tricks and tactics*. You need to sharpen your skills."

Jackson said nothing.

"Hey, it's a dog-eat-dog world out there."

Why did people always say that? Jackson had never known a single dog who ate another dog. On the other hand, he'd seen plenty of people get pretty carnivorous toward other people. Take his father, for example. He dreaded the thought, but no doubt he would have to tell him about today's disastrous meeting. Walt would drag it out of him.

Keith broke the silence. "Ever tell you what happened when I went to court over my leg?"

Jackson frowned. "I thought you said it never went to court."

Keith squinted into the distance (looking at who knew what) and nodded. "Huh. So you *were* listening. You're smarter'n you look, doggie boy, you know that?"

Jackson ignored his friend's sparring. "So what happened when you *didn't* go to court over your leg?"

"As a matter of fact," said Keith, "we were indeed all prepared to go. Court date set and everything. We'd hit an impasse. A stalemate. The city wouldn't go above X. I wouldn't come down to anything less than Y."

He stopped for a moment, threw another handful of dirt, and then walked on, as if he'd finished the story.

"You're going to make me sit up and beg, aren't you," said Jackson. "Okay, I'm asking: So what happened?"

Keith grinned broadly. He was missing several teeth, but those he had were all in excellent shape. *Feed a lot of dogs*, thought Jackson, *and you notice these things.*

"Well, this lawyer stepped into the breach and got me a sweet deal, a deal even better than the best I'd hoped for—way better. I mean, *way* better."

Jackson whistled. "City must have been mighty upset about that."

"That was the weird thing about it. They weren't. Not even a little. The way she worked it out, they were as happy as I was. It was total David Copperfield, man. Blew my mind."

"Wow," said Jackson. "Where'd you find *that* lawyer?"

Keith huffed out a short burst of a laugh. "I didn't find her. She found me, you could say." Jackson gave him a look of puzzlement, which seemed to satisfy Keith. "She wasn't *my* lawyer, man. She was *theirs*. And she wasn't exactly a lawyer."

Jackson stopped walking and looked at his friend. "Wait a minute. That makes no sense. So they brought in a lawyer—and she got *you* a deal? How does *that* work? And what do you mean, not exactly a lawyer?"

"She was actually a judge. Retired judge, strictly speaking." He looked at Jackson. "Beg for your treat."

Jackson laughed. "You are an evil man, Keith. Okay, I'm begging. What's the punch line."

Keith nodded approvingly. *Good boy.* "Here's the deal, okay? Retired judge, now she spends her time settling disputes. Teaches this thing she calls Natural Negotiation."

"And she calls it that, why?"

Keith shrugged. "Not the first clue. You'll have to ask her that yourself, won't you, doggie boy."

Jackson had been right about their dinner conversation. He'd barely put the food on his plate and taken the first bite when Walt said, "So, how'd it go?"

Giving as little detail as possible, Jackson described what had happened in his meeting with Ms. Waters that afternoon.

"Well, there you go," said Walt.

Jackson desperately did not want to take the bait, but he couldn't help himself. "What do you mean, there you go?"

Walt put his fork down and looked at his son. "That right there, when she dropped her little bomb about going national. That was your moment."

Jackson sighed. "My moment for what, Pop?"

Walt picked back up his fork, speared a bite, and used it to point at his son. "The Flinch. You should have used the Flinch." He snapped the bite off the fork, worked his jaw a few times, swallowed, and continued. "So it goes like this. Someone pitches you a price, you know it's nowhere near the strike zone, missing the plate by a mile, but they're just testing you, seeing if you'll swing for it. So what you say is, you don't say *anything*. You react. Facially, understand? You just react. Don't make a big deal out of it. Just enough so they see it. Like you didn't mean to do it, but their offer was so insulting you couldn't help yourself.

"It's intimidating. It intimidates them. They go, 'Oh, but

we could probably go lower.' " He barked a short laugh. "You don't even say a word. And they fold right up. Works every time—Every. Single. Time."

He looked down at his plate and went on eating.

"The Flinch," he said, talking to his plate. "Never fails."

Oh, I flinched all right, thought Jackson. Though it had really been more of a wince than a flinch. He'd practically dropped to the floor and crawled under the desk. *Duck and cover.* No, he was pretty sure his reaction had not been anything that Walt would have seen as a power move.

"That, or, you could have used the Challenge. How it works, you just look them right in the eye and say, 'Can you do any better than that?' Make it sound like their offer was so weak it wasn't even worth crediting—like you can't believe they aren't even doing their job. Like, excuse me, you can't be serious, if we're going to have a little joust here, you have to at least hold up your end of the stick. Ha!"

Jackson sighed, silently. It occurred to him to point out that the problem wasn't that Ms. Waters's price was too low. They hadn't even talked price. It was that her terms were (a) impossible, (b) out of the question, and (c) would crush his soul even if they *were* possible. But he couldn't quite see explaining that to Walt.

Walt had been a ruthless negotiator in his day. Quite tough as a dad, too. These days, though, Walt had mellowed a little. Or maybe it was just that he'd gotten too weak, from age and illness, to be as domineering as he once was. In any case, since Jackson's mom passed away, he and Walt had arrived at a sort of uneasy truce and worked out their rhythms of how to live together as two bachelors. Jackson kind of liked having him around, if he were to tell the truth, even if he was not at all sure to what degree Walt felt the same way.

No, Walt didn't bother him, and having to submit his daily business dealings to Walt's scrutiny didn't bother him. He didn't even mind listening to Walt's going on and on about how things should be done, even if it did make Jackson cringe to think about. And it certainly did do that. The Flinch. The Challenge. Just the thought of being so calculating and devious made him want to shudder. *You need to learn some tricks of the trade, my friend*, Keith had said. *Tricks and tactics*. Oh, he knew all about those from Walt. But no, that wasn't what bothered him.

What bothered him was this: What if Keith and Walt were right?

Because he had to admit, whatever he was doing now, it certainly wasn't working.

4: The Judge

Jackson awoke the next morning with a single thought: the Judge.

He sat up, and before his feet had touched the floor he was already debating with himself. Really, Jackson? *Tricks and tactics?* Was he seriously thinking of doing this? But then, Keith's story, the settlement he got, that was pretty impressive. So was he really prepared to go lay out all his cards, spill his most painful secrets, to a perfect stranger? Sure, he could do that . . . or perhaps he could spend an equally pleasant afternoon jamming his fingers into electrical outlets around the house.

He looked over at Solomon, splayed out on his gigantic dog bed on the floor, still deep in sleep—except that the moment Jackson had moved, Sol's ears had pricked up to alert status. *I may be asleep, but I'm still on duty.* Jackson shook his head, smiling. *Canis fidelis.* He pitied the person who would dare try anything on Jackson when Solomon was around.

Maybe he should bring Solomon to the meeting next Friday.

He dropped his little debate, felt silly for even having it.

This wasn't about Jackson and his tender ego. This was about saving his company. This was about feeding a *lot* of dogs (and cats, don't forget the cats) the best food in the world.

He reached for his phone and pulled over the slip of paper on which Keith had scrawled a number at the dog park.

He would leave a message. Hopefully get a call back Monday. Although it would probably take two or three weeks just to get an appointment. Which of course would be the classic case of shutting the stable door well after the horse had fled. But he had to try.

He dialed the number and pushed SEND.

"Celia Henshaw," said a voice.

Jackson waited for the rest of the recorded message to play out—then realized it was not a recorded message at all.

"Hello—I'm sorry. Is this Judge Henshaw's office?"

"Speaking."

It was a deep, rich voice, melodic, with a good dollop of Southern accent. Not Georgia, milder. Memphis? Louisville?

"Sorry," said Jackson. "I thought—I didn't expect to actually reach anyone. I mean, I didn't mean to disturb your Saturday."

"You're not disturbing it," said the voice. "Just participating in it."

"Ah. Okay," he said. "A friend gave me your number— Keith Davis? Retired firefighter?"

"Of course, Keith. How is he?"

"He's, well, he's still Keith."

The voice chuckled. "And Lily?"

"Oh, Lily's great."

There was a pause.

"Why don't you tell me a little about your situation."

"Okay, sure. I run a food company, for dogs and cats. A pet food company. We sell mainly here in state, and some to a few surrounding states, mostly through small stores—"

A rich, throaty laugh came cascading through the phone— Charlie Parker on tenor sax. "Angels Clothed in Fur?" said the voice.

"That's right! How did you . . . ?"

"You must be Jackson Hill," she said. "I've been so curious to meet you and thank you. I love your work, as they say in Hollywood."

"I . . . my . . . ?" Jackson was as tongue-tied as a teen at his first dance.

"We have five cats," the voice explained. "And no, before you are too polite to ask, I am not the city's crazy cat lady. That's my husband. He can't say no to strays and the indigent. Which *I* have no problem doing, but saying no to *him*, well, that's not among my strengths." She laughed again. Jackson thought you could probably spread that laugh on waffles and serve it to kings. "Our cats thrive on your food. Six weeks on it and they're different creatures, so much happier, so much healthier. It's really something. So, thank you."

"You're so totally welcome," Jackson replied. "I'm really glad to hear it."

There was another brief pause.

"So . . . ," said the voice.

Oh, right. "So, I'm in a difficult negotiation right now . . ." He briefly described his situation, the contract he was hoping for, the bank loan looming over his head.

He couldn't believe he was sitting in his pajamas and, sure enough, telling all this to a perfect stranger. No electrical-outlet finger jamming for him today.

"All right," she said after he'd finished. "What's your outcome?"

"My outcome?"

"What do you want out of all this?"

"Well," said Jackson, "I can't see pulling out of all my friends' stores, but it doesn't look like I have much of a choice there. Though I'd really rather not, if there were any way it could be avoided. And the whole going national thing, to be honest, that kind of terrifies me. But I guess the most pressing thing right now has to be that bank loan. I mean, that could just be game over, end of story. What I really need is that contract. If I can close this deal, I'm pretty sure that will get the bank to back off and give me some breathing room."

There was a silence.

"All right," said the Judge. "I don't think I heard any *This is what I want* in there. You just described a lot of problems. What do you *want*?"

"Right. Well, I guess what I want is for the bank to give me some leeway, so I can keep growing my business at a pace that feels manageable."

Yet another brief silence.

"All right. Is that what you want? Really want?"

Jackson thought about that for a moment.

"Let me ask you a different question," said the Judge. "What do you *have*?"

"What do I have?"

"Yes. What do you have, right now, that you love. That gives you joy. That makes you say, Yes! *This* is the whole point."

Jackson nodded, then realized she couldn't hear that over the phone and added, "Okay, I see what you mean." He paused for a moment.

"WOOF," said Solomon quietly.

Jackson looked at him.

Solomon looked back at Jackson, who smiled and said into the phone: "I have a dog. A humongous, slobbery, affectionate, noble beast who gives new meaning to the word *faithful*. I have a ton of other animals, too, I don't mean here at home, I mean animals I see at the stores where we deliver, animals I've gotten to know. I love seeing all the pets our food feeds, and the people who come with those animals, how much richer their lives are with those animals as part of them. Honestly, I love hearing you tell me how your husband's five cats are thriving, and knowing that it was the long hours in my cramped little kitchen, experimenting, adjusting, developing these products, that helped make that happen.

"*That's* what I have that I love."

There was another pause, this one long enough that Jackson wondered if they were still connected.

"Do I still have you?"

"Oh yes," she said. "Yes, you do. Well, Jackson Hill, that was beautiful." There was a brief silence. Then she continued: "So here's my experience: When you're not sure what you want, look at what you have that you love, that gives you joy. Chances are excellent, what you want is more of *that*."

Jackson felt strangely warmed by her words—but at the

same time, confused. How would any of this help him close his deal, nail down that contract, find his way out of this impossible situation?

"If only it were that simple," he murmured.

"I know," said the voice. "It really is, you know," she added. "As simple as that. Alas, though." She sighed. "*We're* not. We make it complicated, tie it up in knots."

That sounded about right to Jackson. Tied up in knots. *Yup*, as Walt would say.

"So, how do you untie those knots?" said Jackson.

"Ah," said the voice. "That is the sixty-four-thousand-dollar question, isn't it."

"Which is where you come in."

"Yes."

It was a little unnerving, the degree to which she did *not* fill in the silences by indulging in embellishment or small talk.

"So, can I ask you a question?" said Jackson.

"Of course."

"Why do you call it, 'natural negotiation'?"

"Why do you call your product, 'natural pet food'?"

"Because there's nothing artificial added."

Could you hear a smile over the phone? Jackson could swear that he just did.

"That's a negative statement," she said. "You just told me what it *isn't*. What *is* it? What makes it 'natural'?"

Jackson didn't have to think about that. "It's what these animals really *want* to eat, if they're given a choice. What really works for them. Like, for the way they're designed."

"Exactly," she said. "You said it perfectly. Same here."

Jackson waited for a moment, hoping she would explain further, but instead she said, "You were calling to see if you could get an appointment, yes?"

"Yes, that's right." It seemed like a month ago that he'd dialed the number. How long had they been talking?

"Why don't you come by my office for breakfast Monday morning, say, eight o'clock." She gave him an address.

"Okay," he said. "Thank you! That would be great."

"All right, then," she said. "Good-bye, Jackson." *Click*.

It wasn't until he set the phone down that it occurred to him what she'd said just before that. *Come by my office for breakfast* . . .

Wait. For breakfast?

He looked over at Solomon.

Solomon said, "Woof," and hauled himself up onto his feet to start his day.

5: The Coach

At the same moment that Jackson Hill set his phone down, Gillian Waters was knocking on the door of a little two-story house on a street downtown the locals called the Row.

The homes-turned-offices on the Row housed art studios, independent recording studios, small publishing houses, even a pottery studio. Down the block there was some sort of vegetarian café and juice bar. Not exactly a neighborhood where Gillian would have expected to find a "high-level executive coach."

On a wild goose chase, Jill? she thought. *Or are you the goose?*

Oh, well. Bo wouldn't be back from her father's until late tomorrow. There were only so many weight-machine reps you could do in a day. Might as well go chase a goose.

The door swung open at her knock. "Gillian Waters! Come in, kid—great to see you!"

The Coach stood a head shorter than Gillian, built like a fireplug. Close-cropped white hair, short-sleeve shirt, well-worn khakis, tennis shoes. His nose had the look of one that had been broken and reset more than once. More than twice.

"Come in!" he repeated as he wheeled around and started walking away.

She took a step in, closed the door, then had to half run to keep up. She was still confused by that greeting—like he'd just reconnected with a long-lost friend.

"Have we met?" she said to his retreating form.

"Of course," he said over his shoulder. "Just now." He abruptly stopped, turned, and faced her. "Wait. You *are* Gillian Waters, right?"

She nodded.

"Okay, then. I'm George. The Coach." He reached out, enveloped her right hand in his, and gave it one solid shake. "Good to meet you!"

He turned back and took off again. She followed him through what looked like an entirely normal (if tiny) residential living room and into what would probably have been called a den, now refitted as a cozy office.

George—the Coach—slipped behind his desk, a huge mahogany-and-leather battleship of a thing that took up half the room, and gestured toward a comfy-looking mahogany-and-leather armchair. As she took her seat, she looked around the room.

The wall was peppered with photos, all different sizes and at different heights, giving the impression that a madman had burst in with an oversize machine gun loaded with framed pictures and randomly sprayed the place. Some were of various sports greats (Gillian didn't follow sports as much as Bo did, but even she recognized some of these faces) and business icons (*these* she knew well, and they impressed her greatly), every one of them posing along with a beaming Coach. There were a few shots she recognized with some of the city's biggest philanthropists. These impressed her most of all.

"Welcome to the dugout," said the Coach.

Several small shelves built into the wall sported trophies, one of which consisted of a gleaming pair of boxing gloves clasped together. Were they gold-plated?

The Coach noticed the direction of her gaze. "I started out as a fighter, and a pretty good one. Though," here he pointed to his own nose, "not always good enough. As you noticed from my busted schnozz."

Gillian blushed. Had she been that obvious?

"Those were my hard-driving days," he continued. "Raised a lot of hell, won a lot of rounds. Went pro for a while, too. Eventually got civilized, ended up working as a high school coach. Boxing, wrestling, football, baseball, soccer, you name it. But you didn't come for my résumé. You said you wanted to talk about the Winning Strategy. Good. Did you say you were a journalist? No, wait—" he continued before she could reply. "No, you're in business. An executive at . . . that big pet place? Smith and Banks."

"Yes," said Gillian. "I'm a buyer there."

"And, don't tell me: you want to buy something, and you've hit a snag?"

He sure didn't waste any time getting down to it, did he. She liked that. "That about sums it up, yes."

"Okay, then." He settled back in his chair, so she did likewise—and immediately thought, *Wow*. That was one seriously comfortable chair!

"I know, right?" he said. "Orthopedic. Or something. Amazing, right? Had it made special. I want my visitors to feel well taken care of." He took a gold-plated pen from its holder and began fiddling with it, as if to keep up with his thoughts. Gillian couldn't help noticing his hands. They looked like a pair of catcher's mitts.

"That's just shorthand, you know. Winning Strategy. The full term is, *The Winning Strategy for Getting Your Life on Track*."

"No offense," said Gillian, "but I don't really need a strategy for putting my *life* on track. I just need to get this contract I'm trying to land. *That* will put my life on track."

He smiled and nodded. "I see. Okay." He glanced at the watch on his wrist. "I have to be somewhere in about ten minutes. That gives us five. So, let me sketch out the big picture, then you can see if you want to know more. Good?"

Gillian tilted her head in a slight nod. "Sure."

"Right. So, the strategy boils down to two words. Positive. Persuasion."

Gillian blinked. Aha. *So I've found the goose*, she thought. At least he wasn't an ax murderer. "Okayyy . . . ," she began.

"Just how is positive persuasion a winning strategy?" he asked. "Good question. In sports, winning is about competition, right? In business, winning is about *collaboration*."

Gillian was not so sure that was true, but she held her tongue.

"So, then," he continued, "what's the key to effective collaboration?"

That one was easy. "Compromise," she said.

He smiled and nodded again. "Smart kid." Shook his head.

"Not so sure about that one, though. Here's what I learned in school: *compromise* comes from a Latin word meaning 'Everybody ends up with something someone else thought would be a good idea, and nobody ends up with what they really wanted.'"

Okay, *that* definitely did not sound right. "Which school was that?" The words escaped her lips before she'd thought about it, and she hoped they didn't come off sounding too rude.

He leaned forward and intoned, "The University of Obdurate Adversities." He noted her puzzled look with satisfaction and nodded. "Ha. Aka, School of Hard Knocks. There's no such Latin word, of course, I made that up. But it's pretty much the truth."

Gillian laughed despite herself. She had to admit, it *was* a pretty good definition. When she and Bo's father split up, the lawyers had talked on and on about the need to "come to a reasonable compromise"—and the Coach's definition did in fact accurately describe what they both ended up with.

"So, persuasion," she said. "How so?"

"Persuasion," he said, "is the substance of collaboration.

"You take two people, any number, really, but for now we'll just say two, who are not entirely in the same place. Okay? So, for them to come together, at least one is going to have to do some persuading to get the other side to shift their position. At *least* one, and probably both, if you want to know the truth."

"Forgive me," said Gillian, "but how is that different from outright manipulation?"

He pointed at her with his pen and nodded. "That's an

excellent point. How, indeed. They're cousins, in a way. Only they're *opposite* cousins. Similar on the surface, opposite at their core. Manipulation is about getting someone to do what you want them to. For your reasons. Persuasion is getting someone to do what *they* want to do, for *their* reasons.

"Take coaching. I meet for twelve weeks with a team of fourteen-year-old boys on the baseball field. Most of what I do, frankly, is persuasion. These kids *want* to play ball. They want to play a good game, a great game. They want to improve, to excel, to become their best selves. Right? They want *all* that. But it doesn't happen, not unless I'm there. Why not? Because there's a lot of stuff that gets in the way.

"Most of coaching is just removing the stuff that gets in the way, and reminding them of what they wanted to do in the first place."

Gillian thought about her work with Katie. Was that what Katie did? Just remove stuff in the way—like her excuses?

"Excuses, for example," said the Coach. (Scary, how the guy could read your mind.) "Lack of esteem. Bad habits. Less-than-ideal health. Good old-fashioned laziness. Distractions. Temper. Worrying. All that stuff gets in the way." He shrugged. "I take it out. Coaching. Persuasion.

"Now if I were trying to get these kids to become child soldiers, take up weapons, and go wipe out the city, I think we'd probably agree that that would qualify as manipulation. But that's not what they signed up for. I help them to do what they signed up for.

"A manipulator can have employees, but never a team. Customers, but seldom loyal or long-lasting ones. Friends and family, but rarely relationships that are genuinely happy and fulfilling, because those who manipulate are, whether by nature or simply by habit, guarded, suspicious, filled with resentment, and how can you be happy when that's your constant state?"

Wow, thought Gillian. *Did he just describe Craig to a* T, *or what?*

"Persuaders and manipulators are both skillful at reading other people, and they both use that skill to influence others. The difference is, manipulators seek to influence for their own gain only, while a positive persuader uses it to the *other* person's gain, too, and not just their own."

"How do you know the difference?"

He nodded. "Right. So, there's something a manipulator will do that a positive persuader will *never* do. A manipulator will play on your negative emotions in order to elicit your compliance. If you don't play ball, they'll try to make you feel silly, or foolish, or guilty, naïve, selfish, or whatever other negative emotion will work in the situation. They'll push whatever buttons they can find that will make you squirm and want to cry uncle."

Gillian cringed inwardly. *Push whatever buttons they can find to make you cry uncle.* She hadn't felt great about making Jackson Hill wait an extra eleven minutes for their meeting. And then, using that "Mr. Hall" ploy to keep him on the defensive? That felt downright creepy—but she'd needed to make the meeting work, right?

Maybe it wasn't only Craig whom the Coach was describing.

The Coach spoke this next so softly that it almost felt as if he were just *thinking* the words to her.

"This is not necessarily malicious," he said. "People often do this with the best of intentions. Trying to get you to do something they genuinely think you ought to do—that you'll appreciate doing. That will benefit you. They're just resorting to manipulation because they don't know any other way."

Gillian was looking down at her hands. "But it works," she said quietly.

"Yes?" he said. "Yes. Sometimes. In the moment. Even for a time. But not in the long run. Never in the long run.

"Manipulation might sometimes win the game, but it never *wins* the game."

She looked up, directly into his unblinking eyes. "I'm sorry, but I have absolutely no idea what that means."

Although she felt that she *did* know, too, in a way she most definitely could not have explained.

The Coach looked at her for a moment, then reached out one of his baseball-mitt hands and placed it palm down on the desk between them. The gesture oddly moved her, though she did not know why. It was a gesture that seemed to say, Here, I'm meeting you halfway; I'm willing to offer my help, but only if you want it. And I am safe.

Definitely not an ax murderer, Gillian thought.

The Coach glanced again at his watch and stood up. "Gotta go." He looked at her. "So?"

Then you can see if you want to know more, he'd said. Time for her answer.

She nodded, uncertainly. "I have to admit, you've got my curiosity going. But, executive coaching . . ."

He held both hands up, palms facing her in a *Hold it right there* gesture. "Not actual coaching. For now, just a quick map of the territory. First thing Monday?"

Gillian's heart sank as reality seeped back in with the word *Monday*. "I'm—I'm sorry, I have such a totally full day, I don't see—"

"What if you swing by early, on your way to work. Eight, maybe? We'll meet at the juice bar down the block. Last building on the Row."

Gillian shrugged. "Sure, I mean, I guess . . ." There was no way she could afford to be late for work Monday, but how could she refuse his generous offer?

"You won't be late," said the Coach. "Five minutes. Five minutes and a delicious glass of fresh-squeezed juice. Best deal ever. You're buying, I'm talking."

She laughed. "You're very persuasive, George." What she was thinking was, *Five minutes? What can we possibly accomplish in five minutes?*

He smiled. "I can count everything I know about winning in business on the fingers of one hand. And yes, I can share that with you in five minutes." He held up his right index finger. "Or at least a finger's worth."

Scary, she thought, how the guy really *could* read your mind.

"The thing is," added the Coach, "once you learn about the Winning Strategy, you won't be able to *unlearn* it. And it'll change how you think. Do you want that?"

"Of course," replied Gillian, though as she thanked him and exited the little building, she wondered: *Did* she?

6: Master Your Emotions

Monday morning at eight on the dot, Gillian strode through the last door on the Row under a sign that read THE JUICE CABOOSE and immediately wondered if she'd made a mistake.

George, the Coach, stood leaning up against the juice bar chatting with a scruffily dressed patron. Gillian herself, decked out in an immaculate suit, silk floral scarf, crisp cuffs, and classy pumps, dressed as she always did for work, was looking like a consummate professional. George was in sweats. He looked like he was ready to hang out here all day, chatting away.

Gillian groaned. She'd *never* get out of here in time for work.

The Coach raised one catcher's-mitt hand in greeting, gave a big grin, and pointed at his watch. "We have four minutes and forty-five seconds left," he called out.

A few blocks away, Jackson Hill stood uncertainly on the sidewalk, gazing at the storefront entrance and checking the address for the third time. *Come by my office*, the Judge had said. This was definitely the address she'd given him, but he saw no hint of any kind of office building. He'd thought the address was familiar when she gave it to him, and now he knew why. He'd been here before, of course; who hadn't?

He looked up again at the sign over the door. There was the iconic huge letter *R*, and underneath it three words that had in the past decade become recognizable around the globe:

RACHEL'S FAMOUS COFFEE

This is weird, he thought. Where was her office, in some space *above* the restaurant? Or out back? But he didn't see any other entrance or sign indicating either one.

Maybe someone in the place could help him. He hoped so.

He stepped inside.

Briefly scanning the menu emblazoned high on the wall of the Juice Caboose, Gillian chose a glass of carrot, beet, and apple, with spirulina and an "energy shot," whatever that was. She also asked for an espresso chaser, but the server looked blank and said, "What?" "Never mind," said Gillian.

The server asked the Coach for his order. "Celery juice," he said. "Just celery." He gestured down the counter toward the back of the place and said to Gillian, "Let's sit over there. Out of the way."

Gillian paid for their juices, then followed to where he had taken the last seat, way at the end of the counter. The Coach took a long pull on his glass, draining it nearly to the bottom. He looked like he'd done this a thousand times: a fighter cozying up to the bar after a tough match, tossing back shots. Of celery juice.

He set the glass down. "So, the Winning Strategy," he said.

"For Getting Your Life on Track," added Gillian.

He nodded. "Touché." He held up one index finger. "First secret," he said. "Breathe."

"Breathe? That's it?"

He nodded again. "Breathe."

Is there a wild goose loose in the Juice Caboose? she thought. "Okay," she said, nodding. "Breathe. Got it."

"Let me see," said the Coach.

"What. You want to see me breathe?"

The Coach just inclined his head slightly. *Well?*

Gillian took some quick exaggerated breaths, in and out, three times, then four, then five. She stopped and looked at him. *Okay?*

"No, no," he said. "I mean, *breathe*. Here—" he pushed his stool back and placed his left palm over his abdomen. "Put your hand on your belly, like so." He took a deep, slow breath in and as he did, his hand moved out. As he exhaled, his hand moved back in toward his spine, like a bellows.

Gillian did likewise. Then a second time, and a third, all the while thinking, *Why?*

"Okay," said the Coach, "not bad. Not great. But not bad.

"My first boxing coach showed me an entire catalogue of techniques: how to parry, feint, block, different combinations, everything in a boxer's bag of tricks. None of it mattered. I could have learned it all out of a book—already had, in fact. But he taught me two things that opened up my world and took my game to a whole new level.

"He taught me to nap. And he taught me to breathe."

"To nap," repeated Gillian. To *nap*? Oh, she knew all about naps, and they were a great winning strategy, all right—for when her sweet Bo was way overtired and hitting the wall and Gillian was about to pull her hair out.

"I know what you're thinking," said the Coach. "Naps are what you make your kids do when they're over-the-edge exhausted, to give yourself a break."

Gillian sipped her juice and said nothing.

"But my coach taught us that knowing how to take a short nap is the secret to an even temperament—and to health and longevity. Even a ten-minute catnap in the middle of the day, he said, will extend your lifespan by a decade. I've been doing it every day since."

"Duly noted," said Gillian. *Uh-huh.* She could just see it now. *Mirabel, hold my calls for the next fifteen, Jilly's gotta go nigh-nigh.*

"And he taught us," the Coach was saying, "to breathe. Really breathe, from the diaphragm, so that all the old air departs and all new fresh air joins the party. It's the secret to great delivery on the stage—my boxing coach also taught opera singers."

"Really," said Gillian.

"So," said the Coach, "you know what the purpose of all that was? The naps, the correct breathing?"

"Oxygenation? Better health? I give up."

"Control. Not the forced kind of control you impose from the outside. Genuine control; the kind that can only come from the inside."

Gillian put her juice down. This was the first thing he'd said since they sat down that had piqued her interest. "Control, how?"

"You've seen ballplayers lose their temper on the field, go nuts, scream at the officials, throw their bat or racket?"

Gillian had indeed seen that. Who hadn't?

"Well, the smart ones never do. Even in the boxing ring, in a sport whose identifying trait is for the fighters to hit each other, you never lose your cool. Because you're not there to lose it. You're there, in fact, to do the opposite of losing it.

"So, you breathe. You stay in control—from the inside. And *that* is the key to effective persuasion. You don't lose your cool. You *find* your cool. You breathe."

He drained the last swig of celery and set the glass down with a *thud*.

"That's it. Gotta go." He stood. "So, you'll swing by again tomorrow morning?" He stepped away from the counter and started heading out of the place, Gillian following.

"There's more?"

"There's more."

"I thought you said you could tell me everything you knew in five minutes."

He stopped, turned back, and held up one index finger.

She frowned, thinking back. What had he said? *Or at least a finger's worth.* "Oh. Right."

He smiled. "Let's call it, five minutes *per secret.* So . . ." He held up that same big mitt again, this time with all five fingers extended. "So, five more minutes tomorrow?"

And with that he was out the door.

Breathe, thought Gillian. *And nap.*

Stupendous, as Bo would say. At least she wouldn't be late for work.

As she exited the building at the end of the Row, Gillian Waters decided that her first visit to the Juice Caboose was also her last. She would leave the Coach a message later with her regrets.

She already had enough wild geese to chase this week.

Once the three parties in front of him had all placed their to-go orders, Jackson Hill stood at the ordering counter at Rachel's Famous Coffee and asked the barista if she had any idea where Judge Henshaw's office was.

The young woman laughed. "I do," she said. "A *very* good idea. Right there." She gestured over Jackson's shoulder. He turned and saw she was directing him to a small round table in the corner, where there sat a lean, strong-boned woman with great cascades of deep auburn hair. The Judge, in living color.

He turned back to the barista, whose name tag said HOLLY, and said, "Thanks, Holly."

"My pleasure," said Holly.

As he made his way to the table, Jackson paused to take in the decor. The place was simple but elegant: deep natural wood tones, soft lighting, spit-shine clean. The walls were punctuated like a high-class gallery with breathtakingly beautiful photographs, all of them shot in black-and-white and artfully lit, of children of varying ages. Very atmospheric.

"Welcome to judge's chambers," said that deep husky voice as he approached the table. She reminded him of some wonderful fifties film star. Lauren Bacall? Kate Hepburn?

He took a seat across from the Judge, and a server appeared instantly to take their breakfast order. The Judge ordered three croissants—two spinach and cheese, one almond—and a carafe of coffee, black. Jackson had the oatmeal.

"So," she said. "Natural Negotiation."

"Right," he said. The woman certainly got right to the point.

"Natural Negotiation is a type of contract. Before I was a judge, naturally, I spent years working as a lawyer—"

"Oh, right!" said Jackson. This had never occurred to him before, but of course, *every* judge was first a lawyer, right? "Like caterpillars to butterflies," he mused.

"Caterpillars to butterflies. All right," said the Judge with a slight smile. "Therefore, I naturally think in terms of contracts and clauses."

"Okay," said Jackson. "You're making a contract with the other party."

"No," said the Judge. "Let's not get ahead of ourselves. Natural Negotiation is a contract you make with *yourself*. You can't successfully come to agreement with another person if you can't first successfully come to agreement with yourself. Every dispute is first and foremost a dispute with yourself."

The server reappeared and began setting down their dishes, and Jackson was grateful for the interruption. He wanted a moment to process what she'd just said.

Every dispute is first and foremost a dispute with yourself.

The Judge proceeded to demolish the first of the spinach and cheese. Perhaps she sensed Jackson's need to process. Or maybe she was just hungry. After a moment, she dabbed at her mouth with a paper napkin, took a swallow of coffee, and continued.

"In any contract, the first clause comes first for a reason: it lays the foundation for everything that follows. If you don't have agreement on the first clause, then the rest will tend to unravel.

"In the contract of Natural Negotiation, the first clause is this: *Master your emotions.*"

She paused to take one more swallow of coffee, then continued. A dissertation from the bench.

"In responding to a situation of conflict or disagreement, the most critical first step is to set your feelings to the side. Not deny them, not suppress them. You can still *have* your feelings; you don't need to change them, or even try to do so. Just set them off to one side for the moment. So that reasoned judgment may prevail."

"Okay," said Jackson. "I think I've got that."

The Judge looked at him. "All right." Another swallow of coffee, then: "Do me a favor. Walk me through your meeting Friday. From the beginning."

Jackson nodded. "Okay." As he began describing his meeting with Ms. Waters—how she got his name wrong, how she kept looking down at her papers and not at him, how she made telegraphic little statements that somehow made him feel defensive, *Quite the entrepreneur*, *Somewhat unconventional name for a business*—his face flushed. He pushed his plate of oatmeal aside, put his elbows on the table, and hung his head on his fists as he talked. He wasn't hungry anyway. He hadn't really eaten all weekend.

"You're upset," said the Judge.

"I guess so. Talking about it now, yeah," said Jackson. "At the time, though, I stayed pretty calm."

"I'm sure you did," said the Judge. "On the outside. What did it feel like on the inside? Close your eyes, if it helps you remember."

Jackson closed his eyes.

But you understand, Ms. Waters was saying, *we're a national chain. Would that be fair to our customers?* and Jackson wanting to shout at her, *Would that be a rhetorical question?!*

He opened his eyes.

"Yeah. Pretty upset, I guess."

She set her coffee cup down and looked at him. "The first clause isn't about acting like you're mastering your emotions. It's about actually doing it. Not *seeming* calm. *Being* calm."

She took a moment to dig in on spinach-and-cheese croissant number two while Jackson poked at his oatmeal again.

"Tell me something," she said. "When was the last time someone cut you off in traffic?"

In fact, this had happened to Jackson barely twenty minutes earlier, on his way into town.

"And how did you respond?" she asked.

"Well," said Jackson, "I called him something I'm not especially proud of and would rather not repeat."

Her eyes danced with laughter. "Let me guess. At a respectable volume level?"

"Oh yes," said Jackson. "Very respectable. I'm surprised it didn't shatter my windshield."

Now she laughed out loud. He grinned, too.

"All right," she said. "Can you remember what you felt like at that moment?"

Jackson could, and vividly: clenched stomach, pounding heart, heat rising to his face. He described this to her, and as he did he felt an echo of the same feelings all over again.

"What if I told you," she said, "that the other driver had just that moment learned that his child was on the way to the hospital in extremely grave condition, and he was trying to get there as fast as humanly possible?"

"But you don't know that," objected Jackson.

"No," she agreed, "I don't. Nor do you. In fact, you have no idea what was or wasn't going on for that driver. Your reaction wasn't based on the facts of what happened, but purely on your own feelings. Which are not always entirely trustworthy."

"But he could have gotten us both killed!" said Jackson.

"But he didn't," countered the Judge. "He cut you off, and as far as the evidence is concerned, the facts stop there. More to the point is what *you* did."

"What do you mean, what *I* did?"

"You shouted so loud you thought it might crack your windshield," she said, smiling. "You shouted your feelings out loud, inside your car. In your meeting, you shouted them silently, inside your head. Either way, it's still shouting.

"You were out of control. *You* could have gotten you both killed."

Jackson was silent.

She put her hand on his arm.

"It's okay to *have* your feelings, Jackson. You don't even have to change them. All the first clause says is, you just have to set them to the side. They can be along for the ride—but in the passenger seat. Because if you let your emotions drive the car, then you're at the mercy of a drunk driver."

The Judge poured herself more hot coffee from the carafe.

"When you go downtown at rush hour," she said, "what do you hear? A grand cacophony of car horns—bleating, honking, blaring. It's *the* quintessential urban sound signature, right?"

Jackson nodded.

"All those feelings, driving all those cars." She shook her head sadly. "It's no wonder the world needs judges and mediators.

"Conflict is everywhere. Alas. And it's entirely understandable. It's how we're wired. Fight, flight, or freeze."

After a moment Jackson said, "So if that's how we're wired, what do we do?"

She smiled. "We rewire. Scientists call it *neuroplasticity*. I call it . . . well?" She raised her eyebrows at him as if to say, *What would* you *call it?*

"Mastering your emotions," he said.

She smiled. "It takes time to retrain your default response.

Time and repetition. Practice. But it works. Every time you're successful at responding by unruffling your feelings, it strikes a chord inside. It's like thrumming the low E string on a guitar, and you are a song in the key of E. You experience a sense of *true*ness, a sense that says, *This is* me, *the real me. This is how I am in the world*. And it changes your brain, a little bit at a time. It wires new connections, cuts new pathways.

"In time, you make calm your default setting. And as you do, you become more *you*."

As Jackson thought about that, the Judge set about quietly making her last croissant disappear.

"So, that's clause number one," observed Jackson. "There must be more, yes?"

"Yes." She dabbed at her lips with a napkin, then said, "Shall we meet again tomorrow? Right here, same time?"

Jackson suddenly felt his face flush again.

Somehow it had not occurred to him until this moment: This was a professional consultation. Obviously, he would need to *pay* for these minutes. How could he possibly *not* have thought of that? They'd been talking for close to an hour, and now she was talking about continuing the next day? He was already one session in—was it too late to back out? Of course it was. What would Walt do here? Jackson knew exactly what he'd do: he would wait for the Judge to name a figure and then give her the Flinch. Could he possibly do that? The idea made his stomach clench, but what else could he—

"Driving drunk?"

"What?" Jackson looked up at the Judge, who was sitting

still, watching him. For a long moment he was completely confused as to what she was talking about. Finally his frown relaxed into a sheepish grin.

Oh, right. "Feelings definitely *not* in the passenger seat," he said.

"Not so much," she agreed.

"So not so calm, maybe," he said.

"Maybe not."

They both smiled.

She touched her hand lightly to his arm again. "It's okay to *have* your feelings, Jackson," she said once again. "You don't even have to change them. Just don't let them get behind the wheel."

"Right," said Jackson.

"So: I asked you if you could meet with me again tomorrow, and you had what I would judge to be a mild cardiovascular event. May I ask . . . ?"

Jackson took a breath and let it out. "I was thinking about, well, your consulting fee. I don't know what it is, but I doubt I can really afford it. I mean, of course I expect to pay for today, but . . . ," he trailed off.

When she was sure he had nothing else to add, she nodded and said, "Jackson. If there were a consulting fee, I would have said so. This conference is pro bono."

Jackson's face fell. Was that how bad his situation was? "So I'm officially a charity case," he said.

"Not charity. Pro bono. You know what that means?"

"It means no charge."

She gave an irritated shake of her head. "I wish they didn't use the term that way. Technically, yes, but that's *not* what the phrase really means, and it confuses the issue. Pro bono means 'for the good.'

"Giving a service away for free isn't the same thing as doing good. It's just *not charging*. As far as I'm concerned, *all* the work I do is pro bono, regardless of the fees charged. And I can levy a pretty weighty fee.

"No, Jackson, in this case, consider our time together as a gesture of gratitude from my husband's cats."

"Wow," said Jackson. "Okay. Well, thanks. I mean, you're welcome, or *they're* welcome, I guess." He took a thoughtful sip of his water, then looked at her again. "So, you use your powers only for good. Like a superhero?"

She looked at him for a long moment before she said, "Exactly. That's *exactly* right, Jackson. Like a superhero. Like you."

Jackson nearly choked on his water. "Sorry?"

"Look at what you do," she said. "Look at your clients. Your angels clothed in fur. Look at the people whose lives you touch through your care for animals."

Jackson sighed. "Animals, I understand. It's the people I sometimes have a hard time getting."

Once more, she put her hand on his arm. "Every one of us is a superhero, Jackson. Every one. It's how we're designed.

"Most of us just don't realize it."

That evening, after Jackson had gotten into bed and Solomon had settled himself down (after first turning in a slow complete circle the obligatory four or five times), Jackson took out a small blank ledger book he'd taken with him everywhere he went that day. His plan had been to start assembling data on in-stock quantities and reorder dates for each account so he could begin the process of working out his "graceful withdrawal" from their shelves.

The book was still blank.

He pondered the front cover for a moment, then wrote on the title line:

MY CONTRACT WITH MYSELF

He turned to the first page and wrote:

1. MASTER YOUR EMOTIONS.

Set your feelings to the side. You can still *have* your feelings; you don't even need to change them. Just set them aside for the moment. Don't let them drive the car. Put reasoned judgment in the driver's seat, feelings in the passenger seat.

Retrain yourself to respond to conflict and disagreement by unruffling your feelings. Make calm your default setting.

He thought for another moment, then said aloud, "And remember: everyone is a superhero. Whether they know it or not."

Solomon, by now more than half-asleep, let out a deep breath and said: "WOOF."

7: Step into Their Shoes

Tuesday morning at eight o'clock, Gillian Waters stood on the sidewalk at the end of the Row glaring up at the sign that still said THE JUICE CABOOSE. *You're crazy, Jill*, she told herself.

She pushed open the door. *Crazy or not, here I come.*

"You're back," commented the Coach.

"You're surprised?" said Gillian.

"A little," he admitted. "When we parted yesterday I sensed a smidgeon of, let's call it healthy skepticism."

"Huh," said Gillian, wearing as neutral a face as she could. "Pear, beet, ginger, um . . . pineapple, and an energy shot," she told the young man behind the counter. *Hold the espresso.*

"What made you change your mind?" said the Coach.

"A few deep breaths," said Gillian.

The Coach chuckled. "Celery," he said to the counter guy.

Gillian wasn't joking about that. After their conversation the day before, during a brief lull at work, she had placed her hand on her abdomen again and done that slow, deep breath. It had occurred to her that during her meeting with Jackson

Hill the previous Friday, she could not remember taking a single decent breath.

What she didn't say was that her mind kept returning to the Coach's little office where they'd first met on Saturday, and especially to the walls. Those golden gloves. *He was a fighter,* she thought. She liked that. It made her feel like they were kindred spirits.

But that wasn't what changed her mind and brought her back for a second round of fresh-squeezed juice. It was those pictures on the Coach's wall. Those incredibly influential pillars of the community. If that was the kind of crowd this man ran with, then he was someone she couldn't afford *not* to listen to.

Once they were settled at their spot at the end of the counter and the Coach had drained most of his glass ("Celery juice: best when drunk in the first sixty seconds"), he set his glass down and held up two fingers.

"Winning Strategy—second secret. Okay?"

She nodded. *Okay.*

"Listen."

"Listen?"

"Listen. Not just with your ears. Listen with your eyes. With your posture. Listen with the back of your neck."

"With the back of your neck," she repeated, feeling ridiculous as she did, wondering if he was going to say *Let me see* again.

The Coach cocked his head and regarded her for a moment. "When I say 'boxing,' what do you see?"

"Someone throwing a punch."

"Throwing a punch. Okay." He tipped his glass up and

drained the last dregs of juice. "I have a friend who's a former Special Forces sniper. What do you suppose he spent most of his time in training learning how to do, to a level of unparalleled mastery?"

"To shoot."

The Coach nodded. (Where was this going? wondered Gillian.)

"And a CEO, a person responsible for a major business employing hundreds, maybe thousands of people? What does she do there all day in her Corner Office?"

What does she do there all day in her Corner Office? Those words sent a thrill of gooseflesh up Gillian's arms and the back of her neck. Was he describing the future Gillian Waters? (And how the heck did he *do* that?)

"She makes the tough decisions," she replied.

"Aha," said the Coach. "And so you'd think. But it's not the case."

"No?" said Gillian.

"No. Here's the interesting thing about boxing: Most of it is not about throwing punches. Most of boxing is watching the other guy, sensing what he's about to do. Sensing what he's even *thinking* about doing."

He paused, as if waiting for Gillian to add something.

So she did. "Listening with the back of his neck," she said.

"Exactly. And shooting a rifle makes up a tiny, fractional portion of what an expert sniper actually does in the field. Most of his time is spent in reconnaissance and observation. Which is why he spends an enormous amount of training time refining *those* skills, and not just marksmanship.

"And the CEO? Yes, you make the tough decisions, write big checks, take big actions. But if you're a smart CEO, mostly what you do is *watch what's going on*. In your company. In other companies. In the market. In other markets. In the world. What's happening, what's about to happen. What's even *thinking* about being about to happen."

"You listen," she added, "with the back of your neck."

The Coach cocked his head again for a moment, then lifted his empty glass and clinked it lightly against hers. *A toast to your acute perception.*

"The mistake so many people make when it comes to persuasion," he said, "is that they think you do it with what's in your head. Mostly, though, positive persuasion is about tuning to what's in the *other* person's head."

Gillian flashed on her meeting with Jackson Hill. Whatever was going on in that guy's head, it was still a mystery to her.

"But people can be so . . . opaque," she said. "How can you *know*?"

He looked at her and spoke one word.

"Listen."

She sighed.

"The most effective leaders," he said, "are those who are the best listeners. The same is true for the most effective teachers—and the most effective parents, too. They are experts at listening."

Ouch, she thought. Was she an "expert at listening" with Bo? She thought so. She hoped so.

"Gotta run," said the Coach, and he was up and out the door.

As she gathered herself and got up to leave, a thought occurred to Gillian: *Maybe he doesn't read minds at all. Maybe he's just a really, really good listener.*

A few blocks away, Judge Celia Henshaw was ordering a frittata with diced asparagus, feta cheese, dill, and scallions. "The oatmeal," said Jackson when the server asked for his order.

"You're sure you won't have anything else?" said the Judge. The coffee carafe was already in front of her, and as she poured a blazing hot cup for herself she nodded toward a second empty cup, offering to pour for Jackson. "Most delicious coffee you'll ever taste."

Jackson held up a hand. *No, thanks.*

"Frittata?" she said. "Croissant? Crust of dry toast and water?"

He laughed. "I'm good."

She took a swallow or two of her most delicious coffee, looking at him over the cup's rim. "A man of simple tastes."

Jackson blushed and shrugged.

"Before we get to the second clause," said the Judge, "tell me: In your negotiation with Ms. Waters, do you have a sense of what's at stake here? A solid sense?"

Jackson shrugged again. "Sure. I mean, I think so."

She made an *after you* gesture with one hand.

"Well, the fate of my company, basically. Whether I can continue going on as I am, or maybe expand enormously. Or, well, shut down."

She nodded. "All right. I see that. Now, what are the stakes for *her*?"

He stared at her.

The stakes for Gillian Waters? It hadn't occurred to him even to ask himself the question. Now that he tried, he was coming up blank. "I have absolutely no idea."

"Ah," she said. "So, maybe *not* so solid a sense?"

Jackson thought for another moment, staring at his oatmeal, then looked up at her again. "Wow," he said.

She nodded. "Sobering thought, I know. I can't tell you how many cases I've heard over the years—thousands—where neither party had given the first thought to why the other person was there in court. I mean, *their* reasons why.

"Which is why, in the Natural Negotiation contract, the second clause is this:

"*Step into the other person's shoes.*

"Get out of your own thoughts, your own concerns, your own issues, and step into the other person's perspective. Make a concerted effort to appreciate where they're coming from, what's at stake for them. To see the world the way they're seeing it—which is guaranteed to be different from the way you're seeing it.

"It's always helpful to see the other side.

"If you don't, it's like driving through the city with your eyes closed. You know where you're hoping to end up, but you have no idea what's on the road in front of you. And frankly, the prospects for safe passage are dim."

Jackson pictured what she was describing, heard the startled bleat of horns, the shouts, the crash and crunch of metal and plastic. "Mayhem," he said. Then he added, "Driving blind—even more dangerous than driving drunk!"

She laughed, that butter-and-honey-on-toast laugh. "Really well put," she said.

The frittata arrived, and the Judge dove in. At the first bite, she closed her eyes and said, "Oh, my. The woman is an artist. Incredible."

They ate for a minute in companionable silence. Then the Judge spoke up again.

"You've heard people talk about 'the elephant in the room'?"

Jackson was familiar with that expression.

"The problem isn't just that nobody is talking about the glaring issue in front of them. It's that they're all seeing a completely different elephant in the first place."

"Really," said Jackson. "How so?"

She gave the now-empty plate an appreciative glance and dabbed at her lips with a napkin, then set it down and looked at Jackson.

"Every one of us sees the world through our own set of lenses," she said, "our own belief system, our personal worldview, usually without even realizing that we're doing it—and all the while expecting that everyone else is seeing it all the same way we do. Which of course, they're not. You know the park, in the middle of town?"

Jackson nodded. He knew it well; he and Solomon often took long walks through that park.

"Have you ever noticed the statue of the elephant?"

"I love it," he said, nodding again. At the park's very center there stood a great statue of an elephant surrounded by four blind men all touching different parts of the animal—a leg, the tail, the trunk, and a tusk. "The elephant of Babel, I call it."

She laughed. "Yes. As the four describe the magnificent beast to one another," she said, "each one is absolutely convinced that the others are crazy, and that his view of the elephant is the correct one.

"When I was a lawyer, I represented Pindar, the man who commissioned that statue."

Pindar! thought Jackson. *Wow.* He didn't follow the business world much, but even he had heard of this guy. *Everyone* had heard of Pindar. *Mentor to multitudes,* they called him.

"When I first interviewed for the position as his attorney," the Judge continued, "he took me for a brown-bag lunch, which we ate sitting on a bench facing that statue. 'In situations of conflict or disagreement,' he told me, 'most efforts at communication are little more than one blind man trying to get another to see the elephant the way he does.' It's a lesson I've never forgotten.

"If something is open to interpretation, I can promise you that two different people will interpret it differently. Sometimes *very* differently. And that makes genuine communication almost impossible."

Her words reminded Jackson of something he'd read. "Like Shaw," he murmured.

"Hmm?" said the Judge.

"George Bernard Shaw," said Jackson. "What he said was the single biggest problem with communication? 'The illusion that it has occurred.'"

She laughed again, and Jackson chuckled briefly, too. "To be honest, though," he added, "I thought that sounded kind of depressing."

"Depressing, how?" she said.

"Well, like you said, it means that real communication is impossible."

"*Almost* impossible," she corrected. "And it's in that tiny gap, the space between impossible and almost, that we get to roam and find each other. Which is actually quite thrilling territory to explore.

"Take you, for example. When Ms. Waters said they wanted an exclusive on your products, what do you take that to mean?"

"That I'd sell them through her company," said Jackson. "And nowhere else. You know, *exclusive*."

"Did she say it would have to be one hundred percent exclusive?"

"Well, she didn't specify one hundred percent, but isn't that what 'exclusive' means?"

"I don't know. Is it?" When Jackson said nothing, she added, "Also, did she say it absolutely *had* to be an exclusive contract?"

He thought back, trying to replay her exact words. *We would want it to be an exclusive. Want.* Did that mean the same thing as "absolutely had to be"?

"Not in so many words," he said. "But . . . listen, they see me as a small player. They don't care about my existing accounts. They don't see them as people, friends I've taken years to get to know—they see them as . . . as extraneous distribution points on a graph. An arithmetic problem to be sorted out."

He felt his face starting to flush again. *Who's driving the car right now, Jackson?*

"Ah," said the Judge. "And you know this all, how?"

"Well," he began, and stopped himself. How *did* he know that was all true?

Was it?

"At the close of your meeting," said the Judge, "if I remember right, she suggested you go back and talk with your accounts and 'see what you can work out.' What did she mean by that?"

"She meant they want me to—" He stopped himself again. *Gracefully withdraw from future commitments*, was what Ms. Waters had said. But what exactly did that mean? And was it a completely nonnegotiable condition? Did exclusive mean . . . exclusive?

He had no idea.

The Judge spoke softly now. "You said they see you, by which I assume you mean *Ms. Waters* sees you, as a small player. Tell me, how do you see *her*?"

Jackson thought about the weeks of delay leading up to their meeting . . . about the extra eleven long minutes of waiting in the reception room . . . about finally getting into her office and her not even looking up to greet him.

"Honestly? I see her as an unfeeling, uncaring—"

The girl. That photograph on her desk. The girl, and the cat, with the eyes.

"She has a daughter, I think." The Judge didn't say a word,

just listened. "A little girl, with the most solemn eyes. Looks like she's seen some sad moments in her little life. And is really close to her cat. And what a beauty. The cat, I'm talking about," he added. The Judge nodded. "A Russian Blue. Amazing animals, they are, super intelligent, sensitive. Shy, almost reclusive, but man, do they bond with the person they're close to. Some people call them Archangel Blues, and you can see why . . . ," he trailed off.

"And you see her, how?" asked the Judge after a moment.

He looked at her. "As a mom, I guess." He shook his head slowly. "And one tough businesswoman." He gave a quiet laugh. "And that's about all I know, I guess."

She nodded. "Well, Jackson Hill. Sounds like you have some shoes to find."

8: The Corner Office

Just as Jackson stepped out of Rachel's Famous Coffee and stood on the sidewalk, gazing at the clouds and thinking about what the Judge had said, Gillian arrived at her office building and walked into Reception, where Mirabel was hanging up the phone.

"Corner Office says he can fit you in," she said.

"When?" said Gillian.

"Right now."

Nothing like advance notice. *Okay, Jill. Breathe. Listen. With the back of your neck. That* brought a nervous laugh out of her.

Word around the water cooler was that they'd be announcing his departure right at the close of work this Friday. No doubt he'd be launched off into the blue ocean of retirement with pomp and circumstance and cut-rate champagne, handed all around in disposable plastic flutes, while corporate hotly debated the merits of candidates for his succession. If Gillian wanted her name in the SVP hat, she needed to close this account by five o'clock Friday—three days from now. And she desperately wanted her name in that hat.

She reached the end of the long hall and stopped outside the door, her hand on the handle.

Breathe.

When she entered, he was bent over a stack of papers on his desk. He did not look up. She waited a full minute, until he finally seemed to notice that she was there.

"Sit, sit," he said, gesturing vaguely. He returned to his papers, now slowly shaking his head, and Gillian took her seat at a chair perched by the corner of his desk.

Muttering over the papers, he picked up a pen and began marking out lines. "No," he growled to himself, punctuating each cross-out with a spoken negation. "No, no, no, no, and . . ." he said this last with a note of triumph and an especially firm pen stroke: "*no.*"

He set the pen down and looked up at Gillian.

"Yes?"

How many times had she entered this office and sat here for an audience with His Cornerness? A dozen, at least. Maybe twenty. And she never got used to it, never managed to find a way to feel at ease, never got over the conviction that when she opened her mouth to speak she would stutter unmercifully. Which she never had, of course. But really, wasn't there a first time for everything?

"Yes, sir, it's about the Jackson Hill account."

He gazed at her. A hawk pondering the fate of an unwary mouse. Nodded. "Angels in the Nude." He pronounced it *nyoood.*

"Clothed in Fur, yessir," she said, and instantly berated herself for correcting him. *It was a joke*, she told herself, *he was making a joke*, though she saw no humor in those pale blue eyes.

"Brilliant concept, strong buzz. A good SKU. What's the issue?" *Iss-yoo.*

As succinctly as possible (and without a single stutter), Gillian explained Jackson's hopes to secure their underwriting for the funding of his chain of "kitchens" so he could—

"Why does he need that?" he sliced into the middle of her sentence like a scalpel. "We can ship his stuff anywhere, any distance, at the cost of less than dirt. We already have the requisite national distribution machinery in place."

"It's a question of freshness, sir," explained Gillian. "Local sourcing. I mean, that's central to his whole brand. And honestly, it's better for the animals."

The senior vice president stared at her. Not a word.

Just as the stare had gone on for so long that Gillian felt she must have missed something, he must have said something, he must be waiting for her to respond to something he said that she somehow didn't hear, he leaned back slowly in his chair, steepled his fingers, and smiled thinly.

"You know, rumor has it there's a position opening up soon, somewhere around here."

"I've heard that, sir," said Gillian. "I try not to pay too much attention to rumors."

"Don't you," he grunted. Grinned. Then nodded, and the grin vanished as abruptly as it had appeared. "Good, Waters."

She had no idea what he meant by that.

The SVP flapped his hand vaguely, a gesture that seemed to say, *Whatever it is, take care of it.* "See what you can do to bring Mr. Hill around. He doesn't need any more 'kitchens,' he needs distribution. We have it."

"Yessir."

"It's a good SKU, Waters. Good buzz. It'll be an asset."

As she thanked the senior vice president of Distribution, left the Corner Office, and made the long trek down the hall to her own office, Gillian Waters had just one thought:

Is that me, thirty years from now?

"Sure, that's fine. Ten o'clock. Yup. Thanks, Ms. Waters." Jackson Hill clicked off, set his phone down, and frowned. Another meeting? So soon?

All that day Jackson worried about it. He tried not to, but it was like working a sore tooth with your tongue: he couldn't stop himself.

The moment he sat down to dinner that evening Walt dragged it out of him. How was the deal going? It was going fine, Pop. Really? Didn't sound fine. What happened today? Well, he'd been summoned for a second meeting—not the Friday meeting, that was still on, but an interim meeting. Why? Jackson didn't know. Something must be up.

"Of course something's up," said Walt. "She went and talked to Mr. Corner Office, that's what's up. Now she's going to corner *you*. Ha!" He chuckled at his own joke.

"See," he said, and he popped a bite in his mouth and worked his jaw.

This was one of Walt's favorite conversational tactics. He would start a sentence with just a word or two—"See" or "Thing is" or "That said"—and then he had the table locked down. You couldn't say anything yourself, no matter how long he paused at that point to eat, drink, or whatever, because if you did, you'd be interrupting.

Jackson waited.

"See," Walt said again after another bite or two, "you told her you didn't need the company's actual backing, just their underwriting. That was a tactical mistake. You never tell 'em what you actually want. That's suicide.

"You need to use the Compromise. Tell them that you need—absolutely, positively, nonnegotiably *must have*—something that's way more than what you're really looking for. You want to walk out of there with the moon? Tell 'em you need the whole solar system, nothing less will work. Knowing they'll say, 'Listen, we can't do the solar system; best we can do is the planet Earth,' and when they do, and you say, now all generous and agreeable, 'Hey, I want to work with you here, let's split the difference, just throw in the moon as a gesture of goodwill, and me and my people, we'll figure out how to make it work without all those other planets.' You make 'em feel like you're meeting them halfway, when what's really happened is, you've maneuvered them into giving you what you wanted in the first place."

Jackson said something halfway between an agreement and an argument, but it didn't really matter what. Walt wasn't listening. He was chewing, gazing off at nothing. Jackson knew that look. He was reliving his glory days.

"Then there's the Stall," he continued. "You find reasons to keep the process moving along—slowly, slowly, stumbling block by stumbling block, meanwhile you're waiting till the last possible minute to make your biggest ask. The more you can string someone along, the more they feel invested in the deal and the more likely they'll succumb to any last-minute demands, unfair as they may be. 'I can't believe they're pulling this on me at the last minute, but I've been working on getting this sale for six months now, and it's not worth losing all that time, energy, and effort.' So they give in."

Now he refocused on Jackson.

"Of course, that only works when you can afford to invest the time. You can't. Fact is, it sounds like she already used the Stall on *you*. So forget that one."

He stabbed another bite of dinner, chewed, and swallowed.

"You're in a tight spot."

Stab. Chew, swallow. Stab—and he pointed his fork-pinioned bite at Jackson.

"What you need is the Takeaway. You make it clear that your terms are more than fair, and if they can't meet you there, you'll have to take the offer off the table—and that you have no problem walking away from the deal. Which of course you have absolutely no intention of doing, but they don't know that."

"I'm not so sure that would play well, Pop," ventured Jackson. "If I threatened to walk away, my guess is, they'd just let me walk away."

"Look," said Walt. "They want your business. This meeting wouldn't be happening if they didn't. You think they've got you over a barrel, Son, but you're wrong. You're the one in a position of strength here.

"They're saying they expect you to go from local to national, just like that, and not assume any of the risk themselves? Ha! They're posturing.

"You're in the right here, Jackie. Don't roll over.

"Fight for what you want."

You're in the right here, Jackie. Fight for what you want. Jackson sat up in bed, thinking about the conversation with Walt, and about how different it was from his conversation with the Judge. Strangely enough, though, they shared one thing in common.

They both had made it clear that Jackson did not have the first clue what was going on in Ms. Waters's mind.

He picked up the ledger book he'd started writing in the night before and looked at the cover.

MY CONTRACT WITH MYSELF

He reread what he'd written for the first clause, then turned to the next blank page and wrote:

2. STEP INTO THE
OTHER PERSON'S SHOES.

Get out of your own head and step into the other person's perspective. See the world through their lenses. Appreciate where they're coming from and what's at stake for them.

He closed the book and set it back on his nightstand.

It's always helpful to see the other side, she'd said.

He hoped he'd be able to do that in his meeting with Ms. Waters the next day.

He hoped he would be able to keep his feelings in the passenger seat, and make calm his default setting.

Solomon began to snore.

9: Set the Frame

When Gillian stepped through the door of the Juice Caboose on Wednesday morning there was a young girl at her side, all limbs, knees, and elbows like a baby deer. A baby deer with big solemn eyes.

Gillian spread her hands apologetically. "We're on our way to a riding lesson this morning. I hope it's okay."

The Coach looked down at the girl. "You like horses?"

She turned her big eyes up at him, two silent full moons, and nodded.

"They are beautiful, aren't they?" More solemn nodding. "Such noble, gentle creatures." He glanced up at the menu on the wall, then turned to Gillian. "What would . . ."

"Bo," said Gillian. "I'm sorry. Bo, this is George, the Coach. George, this is my daughter, Bo."

"I'm pleased to meet you, Bo," said the Coach. "Would you like a glass of juice to drink? Anything, any kind at all. Apple juice, orange juice. Alfalfa juice. Hay juice."

She giggled. "Yes, please." She spoke so quietly that she barely made a sound. "Do they have almond milk?"

He gave her a serious nod. "I'm pretty sure they do." He ordered his celery juice and a glass of cold almond milk for Bo. When Gillian had placed her order (a repeat of the pear-beet-ginger-pineapple), he insisted on paying for all three.

They made their way to the back of the counter and took the last three seats: the Coach, then Gillian, then Bo. Before clambering up onto her stool, Bo looked over at the Coach. "Thank you for the almond milk," she said, her voice no more than a rustling of leaves.

"You are very, very welcome," said the Coach.

Gillian smiled at him, a faltering smile, all at once feeling oddly emotional. "So," she said, sitting up straighter.

The Coach turned to her. "Yes, of course. So: on to our continuing series on Coach George's Wiiinnnnning Strategy." He stretched out the word *winning* to make it sound like a horse's whinny.

Bo giggled.

"Third secret," he said, and he held up three fingers. "Smile."

Gillian frowned. "Smile? That's a million-dollar business secret?"

"It is. Smile. But not just with your face. With your body, your attitude. Your mind. What you do when you smile— when you genuinely smile, with all of you—is you set the parameters of the game. You *call* it."

"Okay," said Gillian, unconvincingly.

"You know who Babe Ruth was, right?" said the Coach.

Gillian and Bo glanced at each other, then turned in unison to give the Coach a look.

"Duh," said Bo.

The Coach blurted out a laugh so abrupt that he choked on his juice.

"Bo!" said Gillian.

"Sorry," said Bo in less than a whisper.

"No, no," the Coach said, coughing and mopping the edges of his mouth with a napkin. "You're quite right. Duh, indeed— of course you do. Well, you know that thing the Babe did once, that he became so famous for, right before hitting one out of the park?"

Gillian looked at Bo, who stuck out one arm, forefinger pointing.

"Exactly," said the Coach. "Before he made his move, he told everyone exactly what was going to happen. He set the parameters of the game. He *called* it.

"Jack Nicklaus, the golfer, used to say ninety percent of golf is preparing and lining up the shot. And that doesn't just work for golf; it's also true in any kind of human interaction. Which includes business—because *all* business is nothing but human interaction."

Bo was tugging on Gillian's arm quietly.

"What is it, Bo-bird?" said Gillian. Bo pulled her mother's shoulder down so she could whisper in her ear. Gillian pointed toward the rear of the place. "Right back there."

Without a word, Bo slipped down off her stool and walked back to where the restrooms were located.

"Old soul," said the Coach, a comment that caught Gillian by surprise.

"Yeah, well," she said. "She's been through a lot." She

sipped at her beverage, her eyes on the restroom door. "Bo was five years old when her father and I split up. It was really hard on her." *On both of us*, she didn't add.

"Just a few days after we moved into the place we have now, a stray cat showed up in our backyard. Poor thing was nothing but skin and bones. Within a few weeks, that skinny little cat had glommed on to Bo like superglue. They became inseparable. Bo wanted to name her Cleopatra, only she said it Cleo*catra*, and the name stuck. As she got older she eventually realized she had gotten the name wrong, but Cleocatra it is to this day."

The Coach chuckled.

"That cat was Bo's companion and greatest comfort during those hard years. As Bo grew up, so did Cleo. I let her sleep on Bo's bed every night. Some nights she licked the tears from Bo's face." Gillian's voice wobbled slightly. "Some nights she just listened while Bo told her what had happened that day. I heard her through the door." She said this last so apologetically that the Coach nodded, as if to say, *That's all right; you weren't violating her privacy*.

"At night while Bo was sleeping Cleo would slip up to her pillow and settle in by her head. Sometimes she would lick her hair while she was asleep, so that when Bo came out for breakfast her hair would be sticking out like a Mohawk."

The Coach chuckled again.

Just then Bo reappeared. Gillian looked at her, questioning wordlessly: *Everything all right?* Bo nodded as she climbed up on her stool.

"Your mom and I were just talking about Cleocatra," said the Coach, "and what good friends you two are."

Bo turned her eyes to the Coach and nodded solemnly. "Cleo is the best. She found us when she was little."

"Your mom told me," replied the Coach. "Said she was skinny and hungry."

Bo now turned her eyes back on Gillian. *You tell it.*

"She looked like she hadn't eaten in days," said Gillian. "Hiding in the bushes, jumping at every sound. She wouldn't even take water from the paper bowl we set out, as long as we were nearby. We left it there, and once we were gone she crept out and drank a little."

Gillian's voice caught. Why was she getting so emotional?

"Then you tried to feed her," Bo prompted.

Gillian nodded and went on. "As long as I was around, she'd have nothing to do with it. When I walked away, she would eventually slip out to eat. I started placing the bowl closer and closer to our back door. As long as I didn't get too close and she knew she had room to escape, she'd eat. Within a week she ventured onto the patio to eat, as long as we were on the other side of the glass door and left the patio door itself open. As she ate, she would constantly dart her eyes back to that door, making sure it was still open.

"A week after that, she actually slipped inside the house to eat, right at the edge of the open glass door. Then she let me stand at the door near her—as long as I kept it open.

"One day I thought I'd see if she might be okay with my closing the door. I moved very, very slowly—but the moment I began to slide the door closed, she stopped eating and looked like she was about to rip out of there at the speed of light. I immediately opened the door again, as wide as it would go."

She paused.

"And she stood still," Bo whispered.

Gillian nodded. "She did. She stood there like a statue for what seemed like an hour. So did I. And then, finally, she relaxed and went back to eating. After a few more tries, I was able to close the door. She's been part of our family ever since."

Gillian stopped talking, not trusting her voice. Suddenly she felt self-conscious. Hadn't they already taken up way more than five minutes?

"I'm sorry. I'm going on and on . . ."

"You called it," said the Coach.

Gillian looked at him, uncomprehending.

"Like the Babe, pointing at the fence. You pointed at the door. Set the parameters of the game. Made the cat feel safe."

"Cleo," whispered Bo.

The Coach nodded. "Yes, Cleo. You made Cleo feel safe. She didn't want to leave, she just wanted to know she *could* leave. So long as she had a back door to escape through, she was fine."

He paused.

"Remember what I said about collaboration, a few days ago?"

Gillian replied without hesitation: "Winning in business is

about collaboration. And the substance of collaboration is persuasion."

The Coach's eyebrows shot up. "Good memory."

A smile touched the corners of Gillian's mouth. "I was listening."

He touched two fingers to his forehead in a salute. *Touché.* "Well, there's more. The substance of persuasion, is influence. Genuine influence.

"Because all of this—negotiation, persuasion, solving problems, winning in business—ultimately, at its core, is all about *influence.*

"And as a dear friend of mine says, the substance of influence is *pull*. Not *push*.

"If you want to persuade, don't push. Don't confront. And don't shut the patio door. Never box the other person into a corner, where they feel they have no choice. Where they feel they *have* to agree with your point of view. Because then, of course, they never will.

"Always leave a back door open."

Gillian thought back to her meeting with Jackson Hill. He had looked as spooked as poor starving little Cleo. Had she given him a back door?

Which reminded her: Bo had a horseback lesson to get to—and she had a meeting with Mr. Hill.

"We should go," she said, and stood up.

Bo slipped off her stool, looked up at the Coach, and said, "She was smiling."

"Mmm?" said the Coach.

"My mom. With Cleo."

A soft smile stole over the Coach's face. He crouched down to get eye level with the girl (which for the Coach didn't take much of a crouch) and said, "You are absolutely right."

He looked up at Gillian. "Smart girl."

Gillian gave a puzzled frown.

"When you left that door open?" he said. "That was you, smiling."

Jackson was not smiling, not at all, and the Judge had noticed this right away.

She was having the huevos rancheros ("Unbelievable," was her murmured assessment), and he was having, of course, the oatmeal. Or, not having it.

The Judge was just starting to walk Jackson through the third clause of Natural Negotiation, but she sensed he was only half listening. He seemed vaguely unsettled, even irritable. Perhaps, she thought, there'd be an opportunity to ask about that. Perhaps. She would have to wait and see.

She continued with her dissertation from the bench.

"Set the frame," repeated Jackson.

"Set the frame," the Judge said again. "That's the third clause. The frame is more important than the content, because the frame is the *context*. Whoever sets the frame of the conversation also sets the tone and the direction in which it will go.

"For example, in your meeting last Friday, who set the frame?"

Jackson thought about that for a moment. "I'm not sure. I think, maybe I did?"

"Tell me. Describe it to me, how it started."

"Well, she asked me to tell her about my business, so I told her—"

"No, before that. How did it start, *exactly*."

"I don't remember, *exactly*," Jackson snapped back. He sighed, more loudly than he meant to. "Sorry," he said. "I'm just . . ." He pushed his plate of oatmeal a few inches farther away and sighed a second time. "Hang on, let me think for a sec."

The Judge gave one small nod and gestured with her hand. *Don't worry about it. Take your time.*

Jackson frowned in thought. Exactly how *had* that conversation started? He closed his eyes and thought back.

Looking at her desk . . . that picture of the girl and the cat . . .

He opened his eyes. "She called me Mr. Hall."

The Judge nodded gravely, as if to say, *Of course she did.* "And?"

"I corrected her, and she said she was sorry for getting it wrong, then asked me to tell her about my business."

"She said she was sorry?"

Jackson nodded.

"What did she say, *exactly*?"

He frowned again. "She said, 'Of course. Mr. Hill. Jackson. So, tell me about your business.'"

"Ah. So she didn't really apologize for getting your name wrong."

No, she hadn't, had she. She hadn't said, *Sorry*, as in, *I'm sorry*. She'd said, *Sorry?* As in, *Huh? Could you say that again? I wasn't really listening*.

"What happened before that. Before you stepped into her office."

"Nothing, really. I just waited. I was there on time, well ahead of time, actually, but I didn't get in to see her till ten or eleven past."

The Judge said nothing.

"Wow," said Jackson, as the penny dropped.

The Judge nodded. "Exactly. Jackson, she set the frame a hundred ways from Sunday. She had you wait, as if she were far busier than you were—that is, more important than you were. When you walked in, rather than greeting you, she kept studying her file on your business, as if she'd been too occupied with other matters—other *more important* matters— to actually read what you'd sent her until the moment you were already sitting right there in her office. And do you really think she didn't know your correct name?

"Or let me put it this way: She had a scheduled meeting with you to discuss the possibility of taking on your business as a major account for her company. How could she possibly *not* have known your name?"

"Wow," said Jackson again.

"Wow, indeed. She set a frame that said, *I have the upper hand, from the very first moment on, and you and I both know it, so shall we just get down to brass tacks?* From the sound of it, your Ms. Waters would make a formidable trial attorney."

Jackson shook his head slowly in disbelief. "Wow," he said

a third time. Then, for the first time that morning, his face did something that resembled a hint of a smile. "So you're saying, I was framed? I bet you heard that a lot in the courtroom."

That deep, throaty laugh again. "Yes," she said. "In fact, that is the truth. Everyone is framed, one way or another.

"Do you know the word *semiotics*? It has to do with the creation of meaning. Because language is more than language, it's also a creative force. The language you use to describe the situation sets up the situation. And not only words, but gestures, tone, posture, everything.

"Some words and phrases—like some physical postures— automatically set up an antagonistic frame. A frame where one side dominates over the other, or attempts to."

Jackson nodded. "Like getting my name wrong."

"Yes. Though you can just as easily set a frame that fosters connection and agreement rather than dominance or antagonism. For example: Do you remember what transpired the first time you walked into this restaurant, two days ago?"

Jackson thought back. "At first, I wasn't sure I was in the right place. So I waited in line for a minute and then asked the barista if she knew where you were."

"And she said?"

"She told me. She pointed right over to where you were sitting."

"And then said?"

" 'No problem,' or something." The Judge waited. Jackson thought again for a moment, bringing the scene back. "No, that wasn't it. She said, 'My pleasure.' "

The Judge nodded once. "Exactly."

"Wait," said Jackson. "How do you know she said that? You were sitting way over here. You couldn't possibly have heard us."

"That's what she always says," replied the Judge. "It's what every barista and server at every Rachel's Famous establishment says, from coast to coast and around the world. And that's not an accident. It's in their training, directly from Rachel herself. So tell me, what have you heard servers at other breakfast shops or take-out counters say when you place an order?"

"*No problem*," said Jackson. "*Rrrright back atcha. Hey, just doin' my job.*"

There was another cascade of laughter from the Judge. "It never fails to amaze me, the things people say. *No problem*, for instance. Really? Should it have to be pointed out that your being here, placing an order, is *not a problem*? Or, if he's *just doin' his job*, how does *that* make you feel? Like your thanks were not appropriate, because he was only doing what he was told? And *Rrrright back atcha*—what does that even mean?

"But when they say, *My pleasure*, it creates a whole different context. It sets a powerfully positive frame."

"I see that," said Jackson. He'd never imagined that you could communicate so much with just two words. But then, look at how much Solomon communicated—with no words at all.

"One of my favorite judges," said the Judge, "was a master of setting the frame. He wasn't officially a judge—he was officially the president—but he'd spent years as a very successful lawyer before he was called upon to preside over one of the worst disputes this nation has ever witnessed.

"Mr. Lincoln had a very unusual style as a trial lawyer. He would typically begin his opening arguments by summing up the *other* side's case, pointing out the positive aspects of their position and how very worthy they were of sober consideration. In fact, it was said that if you'd walked into the courtroom at the moment he was giving his opening remarks, you'd have assumed he was representing the opposing side."

She paused to lay into the rest of her huevos rancheros, her eyes never leaving Jackson as she ate.

"Okay," said Jackson. "Interesting approach for a trial lawyer." He was thinking of Keith's story, about how the lawyer brought in by the other side ended up getting *him* a settlement. Then he remembered that that same lawyer (turned judge, turned mediator) was sitting right here across from him, demolishing her breakfast.

The Judge nodded as she dabbed a napkin to her lips. "Sounds strange, I know. But by doing this, Mr. Lincoln was establishing his credibility with the judge and jury, and demonstrating that both sides had a legitimate view and that he was seeking only the truth.

"When it came time to present *his* side of the dispute, he would really pour it on, offering up point after point, fact after fact, to make his client's case. It was like—and forgive the sports metaphor—taking the ball and running seventy yards for a touchdown through an open field, with no defensive players left to stop him. Because by this point his credibility level was so high. After all, if he was so forthright about the strengths of the other side's position, then he *must* be honest and speaking straight from his heart, right?

"And here's the key: when he presented that other side, *he was being sincere*. Yes, it was clever, and yes, it was calculated. But it wasn't phony.

"Which is one of the central tenets of effective frame setting. You have to mean it."

Jackson said, "Like *My pleasure*."

"Yes," she said. "Exactly like that." She poured out some fresh hot coffee, then looked over at him.

"Jackson," she said. "Do you remember how this conversation began? I mean right now, this morning, when you first sat down?"

Jackson blushed. "Yeah. Sorry about that. I was upset. Nervous about this meeting coming up today. I didn't mean to be rude."

"So who set the frame?"

He didn't say anything for a moment. Then: "I'm not sure. *You?*"

"Me."

"But . . . I don't see how you set any frame at all. You didn't say or do *anything*! I was the one who snapped at you and sulked over my oatmeal. Didn't *that* set a frame?"

"Well," she said, "it could have." She took one last swallow of coffee and raised one finger to signal she was ready for their check. "Sometimes, though, not reacting is the most powerful statement you can make. When you go to your default setting of calm, that is itself a frame *reset*. Or at the very least, it sets the stage for one. So yes, your mood did set a certain frame—but I reset it.

"There's always a frame being set. Always. The only question is, Who will set it?"

As Jackson Hill left Rachel's Famous Coffee and headed across town toward the offices of Smith & Banks for his interim meeting with Ms. Waters, his thoughts kept going back to his conversation with Walt the night before.

You're in the right here, Walt said. And Jackson had to admit, he had a point.

They were expecting him to scale up to national, in just months, and give up his best accounts in the process? Clearly that wasn't fair. And it made Jackson mad.

He *was* in the right here.

He thought about what the Judge had said, too.

There's always a frame being set. The only question is, Who will set it?

He tried to think through how these next few minutes would go.

10: Collision

Gillian Waters stared out her office window, thinking through what needed to happen in the next few minutes.

"Breathe, Jill," she murmured. "Listen. Smile."

She took a deep breath, in, and out, in, and out; put a big smile on her face; then turned back to her desk, pressed the TALK button, and said, "Mirabel, could you send Mr. Hill in now?"

Jackson Hill looked like a man ready to shoot, if necessary, to protect his farm from the hostiles.

As he got up from his seat in Reception, he glanced at the wall clock. Right on the dot of the hour. Good. He nodded once at Mirabel as he walked past her desk and down the hall. *Set the frame, Jackson. Be the one who sets the frame.*

As he stepped into the office for his meeting, Ms. Waters stood up and reached across her desk, hand outstretched. "Thank you for coming in on such short notice," she said as she shook his hand. "How is it going?" she inquired as he took his seat.

"Going?" said Jackson.

"With your accounts."

Right. He was supposed to be "talking with his people," preparing for a "graceful withdrawal of commitment" or however she'd put it.

"It's going fine," he said.

Of course, he hadn't placed a single call. Why would he? He already knew what they would say. He didn't have to "explore" anything. He knew these people.

"I dropped by the Pet Nook yesterday," said Ms. Waters. "The one down on Dale Drive, next to the big furniture place? Talked with Patty there—they were singing your praises."

Jackson was totally confused. "You—wait. You know *Patty*?"

"Not really," said Ms. Waters. "I mean, just to say hello whenever I'm in."

"You shop at the Pet Nook." Had he just dropped into some alternative universe? Ms. Waters was an executive for the country's largest pet food and accessories chain, and she shopped at a *competitor's* place? At one of his little accounts?

"Well," said Ms. Waters, "we aren't carrying your line yet, are we? I have to buy your cat food *somewhere*."

"Wait—you buy my . . . ?" He glanced again at the photo on her desk. The Russian Blue. "You use my product?"

Ms. Waters put her elbows on her desk and leaned forward to look directly at him. "Of course I do. 'Purest, freshest, best.' It's not just a slogan, right?"

Jackson's mind was going a hundred miles an hour. Ms.

Waters knew who Patty was. One of his accounts. A real live person, not just an arithmetic problem.

As segues went, it didn't get any more perfect than this.

The words were on his lips—*Speaking of which, I wanted to ask, just how exclusive is exclusive?*—when Ms. Waters spoke up again:

"I spoke with the Corner Office yesterday. About your underwriting idea. They have . . . questions."

Jackson's heart sank. *Questions.* She might as well have said, "They think you're poison." All at once, it came to him with total clarity: Walt was right. Jackson should never have said he was interested only in their *underwriting* his loan. That was a tactical mistake, all right, a classic blunder. Hopefully not a fatal one. But what could he do now? What was it Walt said? *If you want the moon, ask for the solar system.* Jackson felt his heart pounding in his chest.

"Actually," he said, "I wanted to talk about that. Production on a national scale—that's a major investment. And one that would benefit both our companies. I wanted to explore the idea of cost sharing on that."

They'll fold like dominoes. Was that how Walt had put it?

He stopped talking, hoping against hope that Ms. Waters would fold like dominoes.

Ms. Waters did not fold like dominoes. Not like origami, not like a basket of clean laundry, not like anything at all. All that happened was a frosty silence.

"So let's review," she said. "You were hoping we'd back your capital improvement loan with a signature, and now you're saying, no, in fact, you'd like us to *pay* for it?"

Another silence. Jackson was just about to fold himself and blurt out something, probably some form of backpedaling, when Ms. Waters began nodding slowly and added, "Interesting."

Jackson's mind raced. *Interesting.* Was that good? Or just her way of saying, "Ha! You must be kidding"? He flashed on the Judge, saying, *Step into her shoes.* That's what he needed to do. Ha. Step into her shoes? He couldn't even guess what her shoes looked like behind that desk, much less step into them. The woman was a cipher to him, a mystery wrapped in an enigma. He tried to remember what the Judge had said just that morning, barely an hour earlier—but what leapt into his mind was Walt saying, *What you need is the Takeaway.*

He panicked.

"I'm—I'm not sure about the whole exclusive thing, either," he said. "I don't see why we shouldn't be able to work something out there, too, some kind of compromise, where I can continue servicing a small circle of my existing clients— maybe call them 'legacy accounts,' maybe special-label the line for them so it doesn't directly compete with what's in your stores. Or . . ."

And at that, Jackson Hill's train of thought crashed head-on into a concrete barrier and collapsed in a ruined heap.

"Or something," he concluded, hoping that didn't come off as lame as it sounded but knowing that it did.

After another chilly silence, Gillian spoke up, in that same softer tone he'd briefly heard in their first meeting.

"Look, Mr. Hill. I want you to know, we want your account. We really do. We think what you've done here is . . .

it's impressive. It's, well, it represents exactly what this company stands for. At least, as far as I'm concerned."

The shift caught Jackson by surprise, and for a moment, he felt he was being given a glimpse into who this person was. But an instant later the window slid closed and the temperature in the room dropped once more.

"But you need to meet me halfway," she said. "If you can't budge on these two points, then I'm not sure I really see a path forward here."

She looked at him—not exactly a glare, but nothing Jackson would've mistaken for being warm and fuzzy.

And just like that, without either one of them quite knowing how it had happened, their meeting was over.

As he slipped past Mirabel's desk and showed himself out the door, it dawned on Jackson that he hadn't used the Takeaway on Ms. Waters at all.

She had used it on him.

Gillian stared out her office window, trying to see just where and how that meeting had gone so terribly wrong.

She turned back to her desk and looked at the photo. Bo and Cleo.

Way to go, Jill. You certainly slammed that *back door, didn't you.*

After his walk with Solomon, Jackson dropped Sol off at home and went out to dinner by himself. He couldn't face dinner with Walt tonight.

When he got home, he went straight to his bedroom and got into his pajamas. He sat on the edge of his bed and looked into Solomon's big droopy eyes as he scratched his jaw with both hands. "I should have brought you to that meeting." Solomon licked his hand, then put his forepaws up on the bed and licked Jackson's face.

"I should have stayed home, and let you go *do* the meeting."

Sol settled back onto his big dog bed on the floor, circled himself four or five times, then adjusted his big bones into a comfortable heap and let out a big huffing sigh, followed by a groan of comfort.

Jackson realized he was still circling the meeting, just like Sol, around and around. Only unlike Solomon, Jackson couldn't seem to settle.

He reached over, took up the ledger book he'd written in the previous two evenings, and dropped it in the wastebasket by his bed.

He switched off the bedside light, turned over, and thought about sleep.

Sol began to snore.

Three or four minutes later, Jackson sat up and switched back on the light. He reached down and pulled the little book out of the wastebasket again and set it on his lap. He turned to the next blank page and wrote:

3. SET THE FRAME.

Take the initiative to establish the tone and context of the interaction. Whoever sets the frame of the conversation also sets the direction and tone in which it will go.

He settled back onto his pillows and let himself walk through that meeting once again, this time not to circle what he'd done wrong but to think through what Gillian Waters had said.

What are the stakes for *her*? the Judge had asked. Jackson felt, just for a moment, that he'd gotten a sense of that. *We think what you've done here is impressive*, she'd said. *It represents exactly what this company stands for.* And then she'd added, *At least, as far as I'm concerned.*

What was *that* about?

It occurred to him that maybe she had to go and really sell this deal to her superiors. He'd never considered that possibility. Maybe for her, going to "talk to the Corner Office" was a lot like how it was for him to go before his bank officer.

Maybe her dreams and aspirations were on the chopping block here, too.

In his sleep, Solomon said, "WOOF."

11: Grace

At eight o'clock Thursday morning, Gillian emerged from a downtown parking garage blinking in the sunlight. She made her way halfway down Dale Drive, past the Pet Nook (where she really had gotten into the habit of shopping for Cleo's cat food), and stopped at an address she'd never noticed before, a nondescript door tucked between Allen & Augustine, the big furniture place, and another large operation.

There was no sign over the door.

She stepped inside and followed a long corridor to where it opened onto a large room, filled with small circular tables, around which sat small rings of children eating and talking, in most cases both at once. In the middle of the room stood a long buffet-style array of steam tables, racks with stacks of bowls and plates, trays and napkins, staffed by three people busily serving their small-fry patrons.

Closest to Gillian stood a gigantic man in an apron. He was so big he reminded her of a guy Bo and she had seen on TV just that week, a star player with their city's basketball team. Next to him, a short, elderly woman in a hairnet hunched over a huge pan of what Gillian guessed was sweet potato hash browns. The third server was George, the Coach.

Just then the gigantic man glanced up at a wall clock, murmured something to the hairnet woman, whipped off his apron, and headed for the door where Gillian was standing. At the same moment, another huge man appeared behind Gillian and sidled past her toward the table, where he took the first man's place.

"Hey, Coach," she heard him say. Then, "Hey, Mrs. B."

"Morning, Marvin," the woman said without looking up, as she continued dishing out steaming hot servings of hash browns.

As the first gigantic man approached Gillian, nodded in greeting, and made his way past her and out into the corridor, she realized why he had reminded her so much of the star basketball player. He *was* the star basketball player. And the huge man who had just replaced him on the serving line? Quarterback of the city's football team.

This was some breakfast crew the Coach hung out with.

As if hearing her thoughts, the Coach glanced up and saw her at the door. He waved her over.

Just as Gillian reached the tables, so did a trio of children with empty trays, clearly angling for seconds, which the hairnet woman began enthusiastically serving. Gillian heard her address one as "Master Ryan" and another as "Miss Tameka," as if she were addressing royalty. She all but curtseyed.

The Coach walked Gillian a distance away and began talking with her quietly.

"Thanks for coming. I wanted to introduce you to a friend of mine."

This would certainly be a first for Gillian—she'd never met a football star before. Bo would freak when she heard about it.

"Most of these kids," the Coach was saying, his voice soft and low, "come from homes that send them off to school on breakfasts that wouldn't keep a mouse alive. Or no breakfast at all. Sometimes it's a matter of economics. Sometimes it's just plain dysfunction. Abusive households. Drug-addicted parents. 'Whatever it is,' as Elizabeth says, 'we probably can't fix it, but we can make sure they're fed.' And they are. We feed over five hundred hungry kids here every weekday morning before school."

"Elizabeth is Mrs. B.?" whispered Gillian.

The Coach nodded. "We all switch off. Thursday's mine, along with Marvin, Bobby," that was the departed basketball center, "and a few others. Elizabeth's supposed to take Fridays. But she shows up pretty much every day." He leaned closer and said, "She's kind of a crazy old bat."

To Gillian's mortification, he spoke this last a little less softly. Could the woman have heard? Didn't look like it—she was still busily serving away.

"You don't have to shout," the woman called over. "I may be old, but I'm not deaf. And yes, George, I can hear every word you're saying."

The Coach's shoulders shook in silent laughter as they walked back toward the serving tables and the trio of kids headed back for their seats, bearing their trays of riches.

The woman put her serving spoon down, sat back on a stool, and looked at Gillian and the Coach. "If they don't eat, they can't think. If they can't think," she stripped off the thin rubber gloves she was wearing, "they can't read. And if they can't read, I don't sleep."

She pulled off her hairnet and reached one hand out toward Gillian.

"Elizabeth," said the Coach, "this is the young woman I was telling you about. Gillian, meet Elizabeth, also known as Mrs. B."

As Gillian shook the woman's hand, she finally recognized who was standing in front of her.

The wall in the Coach's little office on the Row.

The photos on the wall.

The philanthropist in the photo on the wall.

Gillian was shaking hands with one of the most admired figures in the city. It wasn't the football star the Coach brought Gillian here to meet this morning after all, it was—

"Elizabeth . . . *Bushnell?*"

"Well," said Mrs. B. "It's very nice to meet you."

"I used to coach her son, Tom," the Coach was explaining, "another boxer . . ." Gillian nodded numbly. Thomas J. Bushnell, CEO of one of the largest corporations in the region: *another boxer*. ". . . And later, when I went into business, she started coaching me."

"George told me you work with animals," said Mrs. B. brightly. "How wonderful! I grew up with a beautiful Arabian. Mahogany, we called her. Such a gentle soul. And *so* intelligent. My best friend in the world, in those early years."

Her gaze, which had grown distant, now refocused on Gillian. She smiled and patted the younger woman's arm. "I've always wanted to do something special for animals. They give us so much love and loyalty, and ask so little in return. Sweet, sweet creatures." She glanced around the room. "Like these little ones."

Gillian followed her glance and nodded. "I noticed how you treat these kids. It's like . . . well, like they're royalty."

"Every one of these children needs food in their bellies," said Mrs. B. "Providing that is the easy part. We also make sure we send them off with some self-respect and dignity under their belts. Malnourishment, sad to say, comes in many forms."

She headed back to the serving center as more kids swarmed.

"And *that*," said the Coach, "is why I wanted you to meet her." He held up four fingers. "A walking, talking example of the fourth secret."

They both stood watching Marvin and Mrs. B. serving their new batch of customers. "Look at those two," said the Coach. "You see what they have in common?"

Just then Marvin bent down over the table and gently bumped fists with a little girl who looked to be about a quarter of his height, then straightened up again with a big smile. He towered over Mrs. B. like a skyscraper dropped into a hamlet.

What *did* they have in common? Gillian saw it, but couldn't quite put a name to it.

"*Grace*," said the Coach. "You know why a cat always lands

on its feet? Because it never loses poise. Take high-speed photos of a cat jumping off a wall, even of a cat *falling* off a wall,
and you'll see the same thing in every single frame. *Grace*. A
cat is always graceful, no matter what.

"A good athlete is like that. Always graceful, in every moment. Graceful in action. Graceful in thought. And gracious
in conduct.

"Which is the fourth secret of the Winning Strategy: *Be
gracious*."

Gracious. That did seem a good description of this entire
scene.

"When Elizabeth started coaching me, the very first thing
she taught me was also the most important thing she taught me.
'Have a kind and generous spirit, George,' she said. 'A kind and
generous spirit always wins. And you know why that is?'

"I didn't, of course. I never know the answers to the questions she asks."

Gillian could easily imagine that. The woman had a sort of
oracular quality. Sphinx in a hairnet.

The Coach turned to face Gillian. " 'Because,' she said,
'gratitude is the secret to all magnificent success.' "

They were quiet for a few moments, those last eight words
echoing in Gillian's brain like a thunderclap, until the silence
was broken by Mrs. B.'s voice calling over to them.

"Same root, you know."

Gillian and the Coach both turned back in her direction.
"Ma'am?" said Gillian.

"Gratitude," she said. "Same root word as *grace* and *gra-*

cious. From the Latin *gratia,* meaning favor, esteem, regard, a pleasing quality, goodwill, and before that from earlier roots meaning to announce, sing, praise, celebrate. In English, its first meaning was more like *divine favor, love,* or *assistance*—typically unmerited assistance, by the way, but freely given anyway. *Grace.* Wonderful, wonderful word."

The Coach turned back to Gillian. "Crazy old bat," he said quietly.

"I heard that!" Mrs. B. called out.

"I know," the Coach whispered, grinning like a schoolboy.

While Gillian marveled at the fact that she was meeting one of the wealthiest women in the state, Jackson was back at Rachel's Famous, watching Celia Henshaw put away a large plate of peach pancakes dripping with real maple syrup and topped with French vanilla whipped cream.

How did the woman do it? All that food—and stay so lean and fit?

"I walk five miles a day," she commented, as she touched a napkin to her lips and poured herself some hot coffee. "It gives me time to . . ." she gestured to her head with her left hand as she took a swallow of coffee with her right.

"Time to think?"

"Actually," she said, setting the coffee back down, "time to *not* think. A rare and precious thing. My golden hour." She glanced at his plate of oatmeal, which he had scarcely touched. "Can't I tempt you?"

He looked at her peach pancakes. "Looks amazing. But that's okay. I'm good."

"You don't seem terribly hungry," she observed drily. "Tough day at the office, dear?"

Jackson gave a faint smile. Wasn't that exactly what Keith had said?

"Terrible, actually. That interim meeting yesterday? I definitely did *not* master my emotions. They totally mastered me. My feelings weren't just driving the car, they drove it off the highway and crashed it into an embankment." He looked at her miserably. "I'm dead. You're talking to a ghost."

She laughed, that familiar honey-and-butter laugh. "A little drama this morning. I love it. So much for the first clause. Am I to suppose you also did not exactly step into Ms. Waters's shoes?"

"I think I may have stepped all over her feet. Does that count?"

The Judge laughed again, and this time he joined in. Sort of.

"Actually," he said, "it did feel like I got a fleeting glimpse of what was at stake for her. For a moment there, I thought we were connecting somehow. Like maybe there was some common ground to find. But . . ." He sighed. "But man, did she push my buttons. I don't even think she meant to. Maybe it was me. Maybe it's just, my buttons are too pushable. I really do need to learn how to stay unruffled."

"As long as there are buttons, Jackson, people will push them," said the Judge. "That's what people do. Here's what I think, though: I think you already *know* how to be unruffled.

You may even be excellent at being unruffled. It's just not your default mode. Not yet.

"As I said, it takes time to retrain your default response. Time and repetition."

"Building up your calm muscles," said Jackson. "I get it." He took a distracted spoonful of oatmeal, then set the spoon down again. "So, master your emotions." He began counting off on his fingers. "Step into their shoes. Set the frame. How many clauses are there in all?"

"Five," the Judge replied. "And the fifth clause is what makes it all work. Without the fifth clause in place, the rest of the contract is de facto null and void. But without a solid grasp of clause four, you can't get to the fifth clause.

"In Natural Negotiation, the first three clauses are all preparation. The fourth is where the action happens. Where the paws meet the pavement. It's this:

"Communicate with tact and empathy."

"Empathy," repeated Jackson. "How is that different from stepping into the other person's shoes?"

She smiled. "It's something like the difference between being a lawyer, and being a judge. Or as you put it, a caterpillar and a butterfly."

She took a swallow of hot coffee.

"Putting yourself into someone else's shoes means stepping into their world, understanding their situation, what the stakes are for them, what's going on for them. What they're thinking. Which is all important. But empathy isn't about thinking. Empathy takes it a giant step farther.

"Empathy is *feeling* what the other person is *feeling*."

Jackson thought about that for a moment. "And tact?" he asked.

"Tact is the ability to speak to that place," she replied. "Truthfully, yet at the same time, with compassion. Tact is the act of giving empathy a voice. Like setting a poem to music.

"In any exchange, business or personal, empathy is the single greatest determinant of success. Not only having empathy, but also communicating it. You'll come away from talking with such a person feeling as if you were the only other person in the world. That's because for those moments, to that person, you *were* the only other person in the world."

Jackson knew exactly what she meant. Now that he thought about it, that's exactly how he felt every time he talked with *her*.

Was it only Saturday that he'd been worried about divulging his problems to a perfect stranger? And now he felt like this person knew him better than just about anyone else on the planet. Except Keith, maybe. And Solomon, of course.

"I don't know, Your Honor," he said. It was the first time he'd called her that, and she looked amused at the title. "Half the time I'm not even sure what *I'm* feeling. And I'm no mind reader; I think we've established that. How do you *know* what the other person is feeling?"

"You may not," she replied. "The truth is, you *can't* always know. But even if you can't, here's the thing: you're both human beings."

Jackson sighed. "The human being I'm meeting with tomorrow? I just . . . I cannot figure her out."

The Judge reached out and placed her hand on Jackson's arm. "Jackson."

He looked up at her.

"Empathy isn't trying to *figure someone out*. It's not about reading the signs or analyzing the signals. Empathy is *resonance*."

She sat back and took a slow sip of her coffee, once again watching him over the rim of her cup. "Do you know what I mean by that?"

"I . . . *think* so," said Jackson.

"It's like," she began. She set her cup down and frowned for a moment in thought, then looked up at him.

"It's like when you strike a chime, and a tuning fork tuned to the same precise frequency starts vibrating along with it. Or how you'll read something in a novel or hear something in a story that stirs your soul because it reminds you of someone you know, or of something that happened to you once. Or how the face of someone you love somehow reminds you of who *you* are.

"Because they all *resonate*.

"And here's the secret, what lies at the core of the fourth clause, what lies at the core of all successful interaction of any kind: you resonate with *everyone*, no matter how different from you they may seem.

"Every person alive is a chime.

"*Everyone* is a tuning fork."

She paused for a moment to let that sink in, then added:

"Have you ever noticed how practically everyone loves dogs? Of course you have—you more than most. That's because they're such resonant creatures. So effortlessly empathetic."

There was a silence. Then Jackson spoke up.

"So you're saying, I should try to be more like my dog?"

She smiled, a serious sort of smile. "No, Jackson. I'm saying you *are* more like your dog. More than you know."

"So Jackie," said Walt. "Tomorrow's the big day, huh?"

Jackson shrugged. Amazing—they had gotten nearly all the way through dinner, and his father hadn't once brought up the subject of Jackson's business till now. Old man must be going soft. *As if.*

"Listen"—a jab in the air with the fork—"you just remember what I told you. The Challenge. The Takeaway. They'll drop like a sack of potatoes."

Jackson looked bleak. "I don't know, Pop."

Walt put his fork and knife down and looked at his son across the table. "These are good tips, Son. Weapons honed in the crucible of battle."

Walt sat motionless for a moment, staring down at his hands. Then he let out a nearly inaudible sigh.

"Though I have to admit . . . I can't say as how they really worked out for me."

Jackson looked up, startled. "Scuse me?"

His father didn't look at him, just kept staring at his hands. His voice got softer as he spoke. "Oh, I closed deals. Lots of 'em. Lost a bunch, closed a bunch. But . . . what did it get me?

I mean," he paused as if groping for the right words. "I mean, when it's all said and done?"

"Pop . . ." Jackson had no idea what to say.

Walt looked up, and Jackson was horrified to see the man's eyes glistening. Walt *never* cried. As far as Jackson knew, the man had been born without tear ducts.

"Did I ever tell you what your mother said?" said Walt. "The day she died?"

All these years, and they'd never once talked about this.

"No," said Jackson softly. "But I bet I can guess. She asked you to watch out for me, take care of me. Make sure I was okay."

Walt gave a short, derisive laugh. "Shows you how much you know. No, Son." He looked away. Then, still looking away, he kept talking. "No," he repeated. "She said, 'Walter, if you're ever in trouble, you just call Jackson. He'll know what to do.'"

Jackson was stunned. "She said that? What did she mean?"

Walt turned his gaze back to his son. "What do you think she meant? Just what she said. Exactly that." He turned away again, then added, "Grace . . . knew her boy."

Grace knew her boy.

"Wait a minute," said Jackson. "What do you mean, she knew her boy? Why would she tell *you* to call on *me*?"

Walt looked back at him once more. "Why do you think?"

Jackson honestly had no idea. "I'm . . . I'm no kind of businessman, Pop."

"Jackie, listen to me. You've got something you believe in.

Doing something that makes a difference. You've got more going on for you than I ever did."

He sat still for a moment, as if trying to put together one more sentence, but then deciding the best he could do was repeat one he'd already said.

"You've got something you believe in. So don't forget that, okay?"

And at that, he quietly got up and left the table.

Jackson lay awake that night for hours. He couldn't stop thinking about what Walt had said, and his mother, Grace Hill, and what she'd told her husband about their boy, Jackson.

Finally, he switched on his bedside lamp and sat up. He pulled out his little notebook, turned to the next blank page, and wrote:

4. COMMUNICATE WITH TACT
AND EMPATHY.

Let yourself feel what the other person is feeling, and speak to that truthfully, yet also with compassion. No matter how different they may seem or what position they may take, remember that they are a chime and you are a tuning fork.

He stared at the page. Then he slowly leafed through the previous few pages. Set the frame . . . step into their shoes . . . master your emotions. That was all very well—but he still didn't see how any of this was going to solve his situation.

He closed the book and put it away.

Bottom line, what Gillian Waters wanted and what he wanted—no, what he *needed*—were a pair of crossed swords, as opposite as north and south. He could be as tactful and empathetic as the moon, but that wasn't going to get Smith & Banks to budge.

And he needed them to.

He needed to walk out of his meeting at Gillian Waters's office tomorrow with that contract in his hand—or he could kiss his business, his career, and his dreams good-bye.

12: Trust

When Gillian showed up at The Juice Caboose on Friday morning, the Coach took one look at her across the room and gestured for her to stay there, spoke a few words to the person at the order counter, then walked over to join her at the front door.

"You're worried," he said.

She nodded. He could see that from across the room?

"About your meeting today?"

She nodded again. She hadn't shared the details of her negotiation with the Coach, but enough that he knew this was make or break for her. "I can only stay a minute," she said. "I really need to get back and prepare a few things."

"C'mon," he said. "Let's walk." He took her arm and they went outside. He asked where she was parked, and when she told him which lot, he started walking with her in that direction.

"I'll take you as far as your car," he said. "The rest is up to you."

It was unseasonably cool out, and overcast. She turned up

127

the collar on her jacket. The Coach seemed undisturbed in his sweats and T-shirt.

"You know how people say it's not whether you win or lose, it's how you play the game that counts? That's close. But it's not just the how, it's also the *why*. If you know why you're playing the game, then even if you lose, you win. And if you forget why you're playing? Then even if you win, you lose."

Even if you win, you lose. Gillian tried to wrap her brain around that as they walked on.

"If you don't know the why," the Coach continued, "then I don't care how skilled you are; genuine winning is impossible. Out of your reach.

"The *why* of sports is simple: *to express excellence in motion.*"

"And in business?" said Gillian. "What's the why of business?"

He turned to her. "What would you say?"

Gillian thought for a moment. "I would think it's different for everyone."

The Coach chuckled and shook his head. "No, it's exactly the same for everyone. It feels different, looks different, expresses itself differently. But it's the same thing. And it's simple, too.

"*You go into business to nudge the world forward.*"

Gillian looked at him. "That's it?"

"That's it. To make the world a better place. Improve people's lives. Leave the planet a smarter, kinder, richer, more whole place than it was when you got here. To create *value*. Which you do by sharing what you know, what you have, what you've been given. All business, whether each business-person remembers it or not, is an expression of gratitude.

"Elizabeth put it perfectly. *Gratitude is the secret to all magnificent success.*"

They walked on.

"You remember what I said about the difference between sports and business?"

Gillian remembered. "Winning in sports is about competition. Winning in business is about collaboration."

He glanced over at her, impressed. "Good memory. Well, that's not quite the whole truth. Winning in *anything* is really about collaboration.

"So here's another baseball question. Sadaharu Oh?" Gillian shook her head. *Never heard of him.* "Japanese baseball star, played in the Japanese pro baseball league in the seventies. Holds the world lifetime record for home runs—that's the *world* record. You know what he said about the pitchers who went up against him on the opposing teams? 'They are my partners in hitting home runs.'

"When you know what Sadaharu Oh knew, you'll know what genuine winning means. And then it'll come to you naturally."

As they reached her car, they both stopped walking.

"Good luck today," he said. "You'll do fine." He turned and started to walk away.

"Wait," said Gillian. "What's the thumb?"

"Hmm?"

"You told me you could count everything you knew about winning in business on the fingers of one hand." She held up her right hand, index finger pointing straight up. "One, you said. *Breathe*." She counted off on her fingers. "Two: *Listen*. Three: *Smile*. Four: *Be gracious*. That's four. You can't hold a bat with four fingers, or throw a football. Or shake hands on a deal. So what's the thumb?"

He cocked his head, then slowly nodded. "Smart kid." He backed away a few steps, still nodding, then turned and called over his shoulder as he walked back the way they'd come: "You'll figure it out."

She stared at his receding figure, suddenly feeling panicked. "Wait!" she called out. He stopped and turned back to look at her. "How? *How* will I figure it out?"

He reached one hand out in her direction, all five fingers outstretched. It reminded her of that odd gesture he'd made the first time they'd met, at his office, when he placed his outstretched hand on the desk between them.

"Trust," he called back. He turned and walked away.

When Jackson Hill arrived at Rachel's Famous Coffee on Friday morning and headed for the corner table, he stopped short. There was no one there.

A moment later, a server stopped at his table, bearing a large tray. It was Holly, the first person he'd met there on Monday morning. "The Judge sends her regrets," said Holly. "She said an emergency came up and she wouldn't be able to make it."

Jackson's heart sank as he sank into his seat. *Without the fifth clause, the rest is de facto null and void.* He'd hoped that last bit of Henshaw wisdom might somehow rescue him.

"And she told me to serve you this the moment you came in."

Holly set the tray down, lifted off a plate of hot peach pancakes, dripping with real maple syrup and topped with French vanilla whipped cream, and set it in front of Jackson.

Jackson looked at the plate for a moment, then at Holly, then at the plate again. And started to laugh. She chuckled, too, not knowing what they were laughing about, but happy to join in.

"Thank you," said Jackson.

Holly smiled. "My pleasure," she said.

At his place Holly had also set a one-stem vase holding a single white rose, and propped up against it a small envelope with a single word penned in neat calligraphy:

JACKSON

He took the envelope and opened it. A small card slipped out:

Sometimes you need to just trust,
and eat the pancakes.

He puzzled over the note for a full minute. Finally he slipped the card back into the envelope and pocketed it. He began to eat, wondering why on earth he was sitting here eating a plate of pancakes.

Which, he had to admit, were delicious.

As he took the last bite (probably the first full meal he'd eaten all week, he thought), a curious sense of calm settled over him.

He didn't know why, or how—but he was ready for his meeting.

13: The Fifth Clause

Jackson Hill looked . . . well, he looked different.

Different, how? Mirabel couldn't put her finger on it. He seemed more solid. More . . . *there*. Like a man at peace with his own convictions.

"You can go right in, Mr. Hill," she said. "Ms. Waters is expecting you."

"Thanks, Mirabel," he said.

As he walked past her desk, Mirabel leaned forward and stage-whispered: "I hope it goes well."

Jackson stopped and looked at her. "*Thank* you, Mirabel," he said again. "I hope so, too."

Gillian felt flustered. She was trying to stay focused on her plan for this meeting, which she'd spent the last hour preparing for. But her thoughts kept drifting to an image of Marvin and Mrs. B. serving their little kings and queens . . . and to Sadaharu Oh, whose face she had looked up online the moment she'd gotten back to her office. As if staring at the man's features on a computer screen would shed any light on what the Coach had told her.

When you know what Sadaharu Oh knew, then you'll know what genuine winning means.

She pushed the thoughts away.

Oh, she could breathe, all right. She could listen, and smile, and be gracious. But she could also be smart and do her homework. And she had done exactly that. Which was why she knew she had this in the bag.

So why was she still feeling flustered?

Jackson took his seat and looked again at the photo on Ms. Waters's desk.

"She's beautiful," he said.

"Oh," said Ms. Waters. "Thank you."

Jackson looked at her, then at the photo again, then back at her. Then, his face a total deadpan, he said, "And the human child's lovely, too."

They looked at each other for a prolonged instant—and then both burst out laughing.

"I can't *believe* you said that," Ms. Waters gasped, wiping tears of laughter from her eyes.

"Me neither," said Jackson, smiling.

They looked at each other. "Well," she said, "shall we get on with it?"

He nodded. "Sure. Let's go."

Gillian felt her heart beating in her chest. He seemed so calm, and it threw her. *Stay in control, Jill*, she told herself. Eyes on the prize. A signed contract in her hands—not next month, not next week. Today.

"I've put quite a bit of time into this, the past few days," she began.

Gillian had a secret weapon. Two, actually.

Some enterprising staffer for the Corner Office had dug up a most interesting little factoid. "It seems our boy Jackson is in a rather precarious situation with his bank," the guy had said. "They're about to pull the plug, and by 'about to' I mean by close of business *today*. Disconnect the life support. Scuttle the ship. Hammer the For Sale sign into the front lawn." She could practically see him drool when he said it.

That was one. And two: incredibly, she had somehow finagled the Corner Office into giving her the okay on underwriting Jackson's kitchens. With stringent (read: brutal) conditions on how much he could spend on a significantly bare-bones plan, but still, a thumbs-up was a thumbs-up. She'd had to be persistent, and in the process had probably devalued her currency in the SVP's eyes. She hoped it was worth it.

"The bottom line," she said, "is that I believe we'll be able to provide you with the underwriting you suggested. For your production facilities. With some terms attached that you may not completely love, but still, it'll get the job done."

Jackson Hill looked both surprised and impressed, but all he said was, "Wow."

"And the whole issue of exclusivity," she went on, "well, that may be a sticking point, but I have some ideas on how we may be able to work around that and find some middle ground."

Gillian could hardly believe it herself, but it was true. This was going to work. He needed what she had, and she *had* what she had. This was a done deal. Whatever resistance Mr. Hill might still put up to their terms, she knew it didn't matter, because she had the winning hand here. Right? And besides, this was the right thing to do—not just for her, but for both of them.

Right?

But he was not acting like a man about to put up a fight. Not even slightly.

It was clear to Jackson that she felt triumphant . . . yet at the same time unsure. He didn't know how he knew that, he just did. He felt his heart go out to her. She was having a crisis here, that was clear.

Not that he wasn't having one, too.

"That's great, Ms. Waters," he said. He paused, not quite sure what to say next.

"Gillian," she said.

"Sorry?"

"Please, call me Gillian."

Jackson nodded slowly. "Okay. The thing is . . . Gillian. The thing is, it seems I have two options here. Go with your terms, the way your company has worked them out—or doggedly stick to my guns and risk losing out altogether on this . . . this amazing opportunity. For the past week, I've spent just about every waking minute trying to figure out how I can make this work. All week, I've been telling myself, *No matter what they come up with, say yes. You've GOT to get this contract*."

He paused again, briefly. "But maybe that's not the right goal."

He shook his head, a long, slow shake.

"I can't supply on a national scale. Not yet. I'm just not ready." He looked at her. "And I can't justify giving anyone any kind of exclusive. I'm just not willing."

The moment the words left his lips, it occurred to Jackson to wonder if Gillian Waters would think he was being tactical here. Because what he just said sure sounded an awful lot like a version of the Takeaway.

But it wasn't.

For a split second the thought crossed Gillian's mind, *He's posturing! He's* got *to be posturing!*—but in the next moment she banished the thought. He meant what he said. She could see that. She could *sense* it. This wasn't a strategic ploy, a tactical feint, a negotiating technique. He wasn't trying to win.

He was letting go.

What do you have, that you love? Well, he had Solomon. Walt. Keith and Lily and all his other friends.

Fight for what you want, Walt had said. *You are in the right here*. But Jackson didn't feel like fighting, and being right didn't seem important anymore. Even if it meant stepping away from this contract altogether, and going back to being just a guy making the world's best pet food in his own kitchen.

"It's just . . . ," he began, then stopped. "I'm sorry," he said. "At this point, I think I just have to let it go."

I just have to let it go. As his words echoed in her mind, Gillian saw her future evaporating. No signed contract, no viable bid for SVP. No promotion. No Corner Office.

Wait, though! She was still holding that juicy bit of intelligence on his bank loan in her back pocket. She could pull it out and dangle it in front of him. "I have two options," he'd said, and he was right. There were just two options here, and hers was the right one. She knew he was over the barrel, and she could push on that point, hammer home what her company's signature could do for his future, show him that this was the right path to take. The *only* option open to him, really. He might just cave. She was sure they'd be able to work out some sort of compromise.

Compromise.

From the Latin, meaning nobody gets what they really want.

Jackson stood, reached out, and shook her hand, calm and firm. "You went to bat for me, and I really appreciate that. It's been a genuine pleasure *almost* doing business with you, Gillian."

He'd made it all the way to the door by the time Gillian Waters found her voice. "Mr. Hill!" she called out.

Jackson turned back. "Jackson. Please."

"Right. Of course. I'm sorry. Jackson." She was standing now, too. She came out from behind her desk and walked over to face him. "Jackson," she said. "I'm just wondering . . ."

Gillian stopped, her mind going a million miles a second. Was she crazy? Once she went down this road, there'd be no turning back.

"I'm just wondering," she repeated. "Could you wait out in reception with Mirabel, just a minute or two? Just long enough for me to make a phone call?"

He looked at her quizzically.

"I'm just thinking," she said. "Maybe there's a third option."

The rest of the day was a whirlwind. The Coach's philanthropist friend Elizabeth was as good as her word: even on this ridiculously short notice, at the prospect of doing something special to help animals—the *sweet, sweet creatures*, as she'd put it—she was happy to meet with Gillian and the young man who accompanied her.

When presented with Elizabeth Bushnell's signature on a piece of paper, Jackson's bank all at once became exceptionally polite. Extending the loan? Why of course, that should not be a problem. What's that? Perhaps, more generous terms? They were sure that could be looked into.

Outside the bank, while Jackson hailed a cab for Elizabeth, Gillian turned to Elizabeth and said, "You know, this is so perfect. Jackson never really wanted to be in charge of the business side of things—which is the part I love most. What he wants is to formulate the products and be in touch with the clients."

Elizabeth smiled at her and said, "It is a lovely solution. The best ones always are."

Gillian didn't know how to put this in words. "I . . . I can't tell you how very grateful I am, Mrs. Bushnell."

Elizabeth patted her hand and said, "You just did, dear." She pushed her glasses up on her nose, peered through them at Gillian, and gave an almost smile, so slight you'd miss it if you blinked. "And why don't you call me Aunt Elle. All my close friends do."

At five minutes to five that Friday afternoon, Gillian handed in her resignation at Smith & Banks. She handed it, in fact, directly to the senior vice president of Distribution, who was so startled that one of his *subordinates* was leaving ahead of his own more ceremonious departure that he failed to say anything but an unceremonious, "Huh?"

"Best of luck, sir," said Gillian. "I'm grateful for everything I learned here."

She had, she explained, received an offer she couldn't turn down—going into business with Jackson Hill and Elizabeth Bushnell. As of today, she was managing partner of Angels Clothed in Fur, LLC.

For Gillian, though, as remarkable as the entire afternoon was, as much of a kaleidoscope of impossible events and memorable moments as it was, there was one particular point in the day that was still thrumming through her like an electric current when she went to bed that night, a moment she expected would stay with her for the rest of her life.

As they'd stood there outside the bank waiting for Jackson to flag down their cab, Elizabeth Bushnell had turned to her and said, "You know, you remind me of myself. A number of years ago, of course."

Is THIS me, thought Gillian, *thirty years from now?*

Well, now. She couldn't picture a more wonderful future than that.

That night, Jackson practically fell into bed. It had been a long day—huge, big in every way, possibly the best day of his life, but long, too, and he was exhausted.

Solomon jumped up onto Jackson's bed, walked around Jackson's feet and over to his left side, where he collapsed into a large heap with a deep *hffff*.

"What's up, buddy? You think you're sleeping up here tonight?"

Solomon said nothing, just hitched his body up closer until he was smashed against Jackson's left side.

Jackson chuckled. "I have a feeling one of us isn't getting a wink of sleep tonight."

Solomon put his chin down on his paws and looked at Jackson.

Jackson turned off the light and lay there. Tired as he was, he couldn't sleep. He thought about everything that had happened that day. About sitting alone at Rachel's Famous Coffee this morning, eating his peach pancakes.

It's always helpful to see the other side.

He sat up and switched on the light again, reached over to the light jacket he'd been wearing and pulled out the envelope the Judge had left for him. He slipped the card out of the envelope once more. Turned it over.

Sure enough: there was writing on the other side, too. It said:

> Dear Jackson,
>
> I never told you the fifth clause. Here it is:
> Let go of having to be right.
>
> But I suspect you already know that.
>
> —Celia Henshaw

"Sometimes, you have to let go of having to be right," he said aloud. "And just eat the pancakes." He laughed quietly for a moment, then set the note down on the nightstand, switched off the light again, and rolled over.

Within thirty seconds, he was asleep.

"Woof," said Solomon.

14: A Toast

The tall woman with the auburn hair looked across the table and smiled. She loved it here at Iafrate's. Best food in town, as far as she was concerned.

"Me, too," said the man in the seat across from her. Reading her mind, as usual. "Although I am partial to the meals my wife and I make at home," he added.

"*Naturale o gasata*?" The waiter had appeared at their table soundlessly, holding out twin bottles, ready to pour.

"Sparkling for me, please," the woman replied. "*Grazie*, Marco. And still for the Coach."

"*Si*," said the young man, who was already pouring. "*Prego*." He nodded once and silently disappeared.

She turned to her companion. "A toast, Coach Henshaw?"

"What are we celebrating, Judge Henshaw?"

"The young man who was coming in for advice this week—I think he's found a satisfactory solution to his quandary. That he's on, you might say, a winning track."

"Touché," he said. "To the young man." He looked at her, lifted himself out of his seat to reach over the table and kiss her, then sat back down. "And the young lady. And her young daughter. And all those *sweet, sweet creatures* whose lives they'll touch. And the people whose lives those creatures will bless. *God bless us, every one,* as Tiny Tim would say."

The woman raised her water glass in a toast. "To dogs and cats everywhere."

Her husband nodded. "Angels clothed in fur." He raised his glass as well. "To Gillian Waters and Jackson Hill and their myriad of munchkins."

"And their benefactor—"

"Oh yes," he agreed. "To Mrs. B. The lovely Aunt Elle."

"And Pindar," said his wife. "Let's not forget Pindar."

The man raised his glass once more. "Indeed. Let's not."

They clinked their water glasses together and said in unison:

"To Pindar."

THE FIVE SECRETS OF GENUINE INFLUENCE

1. BREATHE. Master your emotions.

2. LISTEN. Step into the other person's shoes.

3. SMILE. Set the frame.

4. BE GRACIOUS. Communicate with tact and empathy.

5. TRUST. Let go of having to be right.

1. MASTER YOUR EMOTIONS

BREATHE. Set your feelings to the side. You can still *have* your feelings; you don't even need to change them. Just set them aside for the moment. Don't let them drive the car. Put reasoned judgment in the driver's seat, feelings in the passenger seat.

Retrain yourself to respond to conflict and disagreement by unruffling your feelings. Make calm your default setting.

2. STEP INTO THE OTHER PERSON'S SHOES

LISTEN. Get out of your own head and step into the other person's perspective. See the world through their lenses. Appreciate where they're coming from and what's at stake for them.

Listen with the back of your neck.

3. SET THE FRAME

SMILE. Take the initiative to establish the tone and context of the interaction. Whoever sets the frame of the conversation also sets the direction and tone in which it will go.

4. COMMUNICATE
WITH TACT AND EMPATHY

BE GRACIOUS. Let yourself feel what the other person is feeling, and speak to that truthfully, yet also with compassion.

No matter how different they may seem or what position they may take, remember that they are a chime and you are a tuning fork.

5. LET GO OF HAVING TO BE RIGHT

TRUST. As long as your premise is that your position is the right one, and the other person's is the wrong one, you have no chance of arriving at a genuinely satisfying solution. Sometimes you have to let go, and eat the pancakes.

And, surprise! You may find you have what you let go of.

A *Go-Giver Influencer*
Discussion Guide

Many of our readers have explored the *Go-Giver* books together in their book clubs, business study groups, houses of worship and community groups, or among friends and family. The questions below may be helpful in guiding your discussions of *The Go-Giver Influencer*.

1.   When the story opens, what do Jackson Hill and Gillian Waters each want in their lives? Do either (or both) end up getting that? If not, why not? If so, how so?

2.   What impression did you form of Ms. Waters when you read chapter 1? Did that impression change as you read chapter 2? If so, how did it change, and why? Did you "step into her shoes"? Is there anyone else, aside from Gillian, about whom your view changed significantly in the course of the story? Is there anyone in your personal or business life that you felt one way about at first, then found your opinion changing as you got to know their situation better?

3.   In chapters 1 and 2, there are hints that Walt, Jackson's father, and Craig, Gillian's former husband, may have had an influence (albeit a negative one) on how these two approach their business dealings. In what ways do those influences show in their thoughts or behavior? Have there been people in your life who have had this kind of sway over how you behave?

4.   In chapter 3, Jackson marvels ("for the hundredth time") that he and Keith are such good friends despite how completely different they are. How many other "odd-couple" pairings of two opposite characters can you find in this story? How does that contribute to the story and its underlying message? Do you have any such "opposite" friends?

5.   In chapter 3, Keith tells Jackson that he needs to learn some "tricks and tactics." A few pages later Walt describes one such tactic, the first of five in Walt's bag of tricks: the Flinch, the Challenge, the Compromise, the Stall, and the Takeaway. At any point in the story, did you notice Jackson or Gillian attempting to use any of these five ploys? How did it work out for them? Are there any similar "tricks and tactics" you've ever used yourself, whether in business or in your personal life? How did it work out for you?

6.   In Jackson's phone call with the Judge in chapter 4, when she asks what outcome he is after, he describes his problems, and she turns that around by asking him to describe what he truly *wants*—"that you love, that gives you joy." In what ways does that simple shift foreshadow the ultimate course of

the whole story? What about *your* story—what is it that you love, that gives you joy?

7.   In their first meeting in chapter 5, the Coach warns Gillian that learning about his Winning Strategy will change the way she thinks. Does it? If so, how? What happens as a result?

8.   In chapter 6, the Judge tells Jackson, "Every dispute is first and foremost a dispute with yourself." Can you see examples of this idea right there in this chapter? Can you see any examples of it in your own life?

9.   In chapter 6, the Judge claims that in making calm your default response setting, you "become more *you*." Do you think this is true? If not, why not? And if so, why and how?

10. In chapter 7, the Coach tells Gillian that effective boxers, snipers, and CEOs alike all put the majority of their energy and focus into *listening* rather than *acting*, be it throwing a punch, taking a shot, or making a decision. How would this idea apply to persuasion, negotiation, and influence? How might it apply in your own line of work? In your personal life?

11. In what ways is the advice Walt gives Jackson in chapter 8 parallel to the directive Mr. Corner Office gives Gillian in the same chapter? What is the essential position they both recommend taking? How do you think Jackson and Gillian each react?

12. In chapter 9, the Coach quotes a friend (if you've read *The Go-Giver Leader*, you probably recognized that "friend" as

Aunt Elle) as saying, "The substance of influence is *pull*. Not *push*"—and then goes on to talk about "keeping the back door open." What does keeping the back door open have to do with the principle of "*pull*, not *push*"? Can you identify situations in your life when someone has left a back door open for you or where they've slammed that door shut? Examples of where you've done either one yourself?

13. In chapter 9, the Judge says, "Whoever sets the frame of the conversation also sets the tone and the direction in which it will go." Going through every scene in the book, one by one, can you see who sets the frame in each and how they do it?

14. The meeting in chapter 10 does not turn out well. Can you identify the precise moments at which it starts to go off the rails, exactly what it is that goes so wrong in each of these moments, and why? What could the two have done differently, if anything? Why didn't they?

15. In chapter 11, the Judge says, "Empathy is the single greatest determinant of success. Not only having empathy, but also communicating it." Do you think this is true? Why or why not? In the same chapter, the Coach quotes Mrs. B. as saying that *gratitude* is the secret "to all magnificent success." Do you think this is true? Why, or why not? Thinking of highly successful people you've known, do you see an especially high level of empathy and/or gratitude in them? How would you assess your own levels of empathy and gratitude?

16. In chapter 12, the Coach says, "If you know why you're

playing the game, then even if you lose, you win. And if you forget why you're playing? Then even if you win, you lose." Does this make sense to you? If so, why, and how? Can you identify examples from your life of both situations?

17. Comparing Jackson and Gillian's meeting in chapter 13 to their first encounter in chapter 1, can you identify the ways in which the later scene echoes the earlier and the ways in which it is its opposite? In what ways have these two people changed in the interim?

18. Who do you think is the "influencer" of the title? Why? You could make a good case for a handful of different answers, each one valid in itself. And here's an interesting one: Could it refer to someone whose influence is felt throughout the story, even though neither Jackson nor Gillian ever meet him and he doesn't even appear (at least not in person) in the book? All of which makes one ponder the nature of influence and what causes its reach, and also prompts this question: Do you suppose there are people whom *you* have influenced—even though you've never met them?

Q&A with the Authors

What led the two of you to want to write this book?

After *The Go-Giver*'s publication ten years ago, we had such a good time going on to apply the Go-Giver idea to sales (*Go-Givers Sell More*) and leadership (*The Go-Giver Leader*). The natural question was, "What's next?" The theme of *influence* played a central role in all the Go-Giver books (as well as in Bob's how-to book *Adversaries into Allies*), and it seemed to us that in these highly polarized times, it might be helpful to explore a Go-Giver approach to influence, civil discourse, and the ability to see another's perspective.

In both *The Go-Giver* and *The Go-Giver Leader*, there was one protagonist and one mentor. Here, there are two of each. Why?

The Go-Giver Influencer is at its heart about the importance of making the effort to see and acknowledge other people's points of view, as different from our own as they may be. It seemed only natural that our "hero" would be not one person, with one set of circumstances and experiences and a singular point of view, but two very different people. This naturally led to the idea of two mentors and two sets of principles—different, but complementary.

The theme of the book is about bringing differences, even opposites, together into a harmonious and productive collaboration. Twoness becoming effective oneness. So in the end, as our particular Jack and Jill go up their hill and come back down as business partners, we also get to see their two mentors dining together (married, as it turns out!), and even the two sets of principles (the Coach's Five Secrets and the Judge's Five Clauses) combined as one integrated set.

The Judge calls her approach "Natural Negotiation," and the story itself is about a business negotiation that happens over the span of a week. Would you describe this as a one-week course in how to be a "Go-Giver negotiator"?

Yes and no. We actually thought about calling the book that! (*The Go-Giver Negotiator*, that is.) So, yes, the principles here can most definitely be applied in situations of negotiation, whether it's a business deal, a child trying to get her parents to buy her something she wants, or two nations attempting to come to terms over issues of state.

But we didn't call it that for two reasons. First, we didn't want to confine the book's message to scenarios of conflict resolution; the principles of genuine influence are a good deal broader and apply to so many other kinds of situations. And second, the term "negotiate" is itself intrinsically negative, deriving from *nego*, meaning "the lack or denial of," and *otium*, meaning "leisure, boredom, wasted time." (Denial of leisure = industriousness = business . . . you can see how the thing evolved.) Not that it's a bad word. It's a fine word. We just didn't want to make it our headline.

Today, the term "negotiate" has come to have the connotation of something narrow and pointed, even ruthless: to get your way, typically by the skillful swordplay of clever tactics and catchphrases. To vanquish your opponent in a duel. (*En garde!*) We wanted to navigate a different path, one based on Pindar's Paradox: *The more you give, the more you have*. A way to achieve your goals while making the world a better place. The word that best captures that path, to us, is *influence*.

In chapter 5, the Coach has a pretty dismal view of compromise. Isn't compromise a good thing?

Yes and no. In some respects, the art of graceful compromise is essential; no relationship, business or personal, can long survive without all parties involved having the capacity to soft-pedal their own needs and demands and accommodate the other. At least to some extent. The word, after all, means "to make a promise together."

The problem comes when adopting the idea of "compromise" as the path of least resistance, a fallback alternative to pressing on toward a more fruitful solution. In the kind of "compromise" the Coach is talking about, both parties give up on achieving their own true objectives out of a sense of futility; since neither sees a pathway to a genuine win-win, both agree to settle for a sort of lose-lose.

The classic example of this "we give up" compromise is the story of King Solomon arbitrating a dispute between two women who both claimed "ownership" of the same baby. You know how that went down. Happily, Solomon was able to discern which woman was the real mother, and they didn't have to follow through on his proposed "compromise"—which was the whole point of his little ruse. (WOOF.) Alas, many contemporary divorces, business acquisitions, and lawsuits lack Solomon's wisdom and do end up splitting the baby in half. Nobody wins. (*Ouch*.)

The worst kind of compromise is when you compromise a core principle (honesty, integrity, loyalty, truth, family, and so forth) for the sake of expediency or some other more base consideration.

When the Coach says "Manipulation might sometimes win the game, but it never *wins* the game," Gillian says, "I have absolutely no idea what that means." I'm with Gillian! What *does* that mean?

Let's face it, people do sometimes get what they're after through manipulation, just as it's possible to win a game by cheating. What the Coach is saying is, while that might work in the short run (and we stress that it *might* work, because often it doesn't and the manipulation just blows up in the person's face), it never provides a long-lasting or deeply satisfying win. It's said that crime never pays; neither does manipulation. Yes, a crook might "get away" with a crime, but it typically exacts a terrible cost—on the perpetrator as well as the victims.

Or, look at it this way: You may win an argument or close a deal through manipulation, but at what cost? Gillian could possibly have strong-armed Jackson into signing his life away to Smith & Banks, but if she had, where would they both be now?

When the Judge tells Jackson he has to learn to "set his feelings to the side," doesn't that make you inauthentic? Isn't it crucial to stay true to our feelings and be our true selves in every respect?

We're not saying you should suppress or deny your feelings. Not at all. We're saying just don't let them rule your decisions and actions. Yes, your feelings are an important part of you, but they are not *you*, or at least not the *whole* you, and not even the most reliable or *true* you.

Feelings and emotions can be highly volatile; in other words, they can change rapidly and unpredictably. It's not that they aren't real or aren't important; they are both. But they're not the best aspects of yourself to put in charge of steering your course. What is? As the Judge puts it, "reasoned judgment."

Of course, the reverse is also true: applying reason and logic *without* consulting your feelings can be disastrous, too, because your feelings can often provide critical clues to what your intuition is telling you. Think of your feelings as your board of directors, and your reasoned judgment as your CEO:

yes, you want to consult your board on every important decision, but the CEO ultimately needs to be the one *making* that decision.

What does the Coach mean by "listen with the back of your neck" in chapter 7?

Before we try to explain this, let us say first: Try it! The next time you're listening to someone speak, imagine you're using the back of your neck to hear. It's a weird experience, at first, but an interesting one. It's like you're trying to hear with not just your ears but your blood vessels, nerve fibers, and all your cells.

Which is, essentially, what you're doing. It's similar to the expression "read between the lines." It makes no literal sense (there is nothing between lines of type, after all, but white space). But it does make sense. It's like listening not only to what a person says, but also to what they don't say. What they *mean*. What they're feeling, behind the words and facial expression. It almost sounds like telepathy, but what it really is, is empathy.

The Judge talks about "stepping into the other person's shoes," and that's one of your five principles. To me the phrase makes it sound easy—but how do you actually do that?

You're right, it's a great metaphor, easy to remember and repeat but not necessarily as easy to implement as it sounds.

What if the person doesn't wear the same size shoe as you? Then you literally *can't* step into their shoes!

This is a great question, because you don't want to be glib about this. It's easy to nod and say, "I see what you mean" or "I know what you're going through"—but is that really the truth? Most of the time we *can't* really know exactly what the other person is going through. Every person is unique. In a sense, it's impossible to truly step into another person's shoes.

Yet we can try—and even if we can't place ourselves 100 percent into the other person's perspective, we can come close enough to make a crucial difference. As the Judge says, you and the other person are both human beings: "you resonate with *everyone*, no matter how different from you they may seem."

When the Judge talks about "setting the frame," isn't this pretty much the same thing as manipulation?

It depends on state of mind, and especially on the frame setter's sincerity and motivation. (As Judge Henshaw says, "You have to mean it.")

For example, look at how Gillian ("Ms. Waters," that is) sets the frame in chapter 1. When the Judge deconstructs it in chapter 9, it becomes clear just how skillfully she did it— and, yes, to us that seems pretty darn manipulative. Now compare that to the Abraham Lincoln vignette the Judge describes in chapter 9. The difference, as the Judge points out, is that Lincoln was completely sincere. If you examine Gillian's comportment in chapter 1, you'll see that she really wasn't. She was posturing, to gain the upper hand.

On the other hand, look at how Gillian sets the frame at the start of their next encounter, in chapter 10. This time she is utterly sincere and authentic, and now the nature of the frame she's setting is quite different. Ironically, it's Jackson who *resets* the frame here, and in a fairly inauthentic way. (With disastrous results.)

Finally, look at how Jackson sets the frame in their third meeting, in chapter 13. Authentic? Sincere? Effective?

When you say "Let go of having to be right," that sounds like not having the strength of your convictions or being wishy-washy. What if you *are* right?

We're not suggesting you diminish the strength of your convictions, not even a smidgeon. What we're saying is take a deep breath and put your trust in the greater outcome. Start from the premise that there *is* an outcome that works for the good of all involved. Yes, *you* believe you're in the right. And you may very well be. (Or you may very well not be, or not entirely. None of us is infallible or omniscient.) But set that conviction aside for a moment, in service of the communication itself.

It's like setting your feelings to the side. Not letting go of them, not diminishing them. Just moving them over in the passenger seat. And putting what in the driver's seat? Your empathy, tact, and trust—trust in an outcome that serves the higher good for all involved.

We're not saying you can't be right, and *believe* you're right. We're saying, don't hold on to that being-rightness with a white-knuckle grip.

The problem with holding on to being right is twofold.

First, having a focus on the rightness of your own position may put up an effective barrier between you and the other person and prevent you from truly hearing them or empathizing with their perspective. Which in turn can provoke resistance in the other person and diminish the chances of their being open to your (right) position. And second, it may keep you from gaining new insight from what the other person is saying that could potentially shift your thinking—not necessarily make your position "wrong" but add to it or enlarge it in some way.

Focusing on your *rightness* can, in other words, prevent you from learning and growing. And it will almost certainly keep you from achieving the kind of harmonious concord that the strongest agreements, partnerships, and collaborations are made of.

As Indira Gandhi famously said, you can't shake hands with a clenched fist.

The Judge's "Natural Negotiation" system consists of five clauses; the Coach's Winning Strategy comprises five secrets. Is that simply a convenient storytelling device, or is there another reason for that?

We can't say for sure, but we suspect that both Celia and George Henshaw learned their principles of influence from Pindar, directly or indirectly, and we already know how Pindar loves to think in fives.

We've described the Five Laws of Stratospheric Success in *The Go-Giver* as "four fingers and thumb." "Trying to implement the first four principles without practicing the fifth," as we put it there, "is like trying to use a tool with just your fingers and no thumb. (Try it some time with a hammer, pen, or needle and thread.)" The same can be said for Ben's Five Keys to Legendary Leadership in *The Go-Giver Leader*—and to the Five Secrets of Genuine Influence here.

The "thumb" in *The Go-Giver* is "The key to effective giving is to stay open to receiving." In *The Go-Giver Leader*, it's "Practice giving leadership." (As opposed to *taking* leadership.) Here, it is "Let go of having to be right."

Where did the name Angels Clothed in Fur come from?

First, it's how we both view the animals in our lives. *Sweet, sweet creatures*, as Mrs. B. (aka Aunt Elle) puts it. But it wasn't easy finding the right name for Jackson's business. We tried quite a few; nothing seemed to fit.

Then, while we were in the midst of writing our first draft, a friend, Dondi Scumaci, posted a piece about having just lost her dog of many years. John, whose sweet noble dog Ben was just starting to reach the final pages of his own story, wrote her a note of condolence, talking about how wonderful these little companions are, then added, "angels disguised in fur." She wrote back, "You are right—angels disguised and on assignment."

Angels Clothed in Fur it was.

Jackson's business is of course fictional; still, John and his wife, Ana, do cook their dogs' food in their kitchen, using "only the purest, only the freshest, only the best" ingredients. (We think it's the best dog food in the world.) (Ben and Toby both just said, "WOOF!")

Does the name Smith & Banks have special meaning, like Clason-Hill and Allen & Augustine?

The short answer is, "No, but that was on purpose!"

Actually, we tried out dozens of pet-related names first, but of all the candidates we came up with—from Pets, Inc., Pet World, and Pet Planet to Pets-R-Us, Petagonia, and You Pet Your Life—were all in use by real businesses! We discovered that there are approximately one billion ingenious pet-related store names out there. (People do love their animals!)

So we rethought the whole proposition.

In *The Go-Giver*, Joe's company Clason-Hill Trust Corporation was named after George Clason (*The Richest Man in*

Babylon) and Napoleon Hill (*Think and Grow Rich*). In *The Go-Giver Leader*, the chair maker Allen & Augustine was named for James Allen (*As a Man Thinketh*) and Augustine "Og" Mandino (*The Greatest Salesman in the World*). In this story, though, we realized we didn't want to paint Gillian's company as an especially inspiring place, even though there are lovely people who work there, like Gillian and Mirabel. So we sought to make the name as generic and faceless as possible. Thus: Smith & Banks was born.

You wrote once that the Pindar character in *The Go-Giver* was loosely based on Bob Proctor; are there any individual characters in this story based on real people?

Yes, at least one: Bo's cat, Cleocatra, who is actually an amalgam of two real-life cats.

Years ago, Bob befriended a stray cat, to whom he gave the name Liberty. Gillian's lengthy "courtship" of Cleo (described in chapter 9) is an accurate account of Bob and Liberty's delicately cautious introduction. Bob later wrote a blog post titled "Lessons from Liberty the Cat," about the importance of leaving the back door open, and it became his most popular post ever. Liberty lived with Bob for the rest of her feline days.

When John was very young (five or so), a starved, terrified stray cat—a Russian Blue—appeared in his neighborhood. Adopted by John's family and given the name Chiquita, she did in fact become John's constant companion, just as with

Cleo and young Bo. The account of Cleo sleeping on Bo's bed happened exactly as described here, complete with the cat-licked spiky hair every morning.

It was fun to see Rachel's Famous Coffee making an appearance! Are there other elements from earlier books?

It is wonderful to see how far Rachel's Famous Coffee has come since its founding ten years ago, isn't it? (And you might recognize those beautiful black-and-white photos on the wall there; they made their first appearance in the last chapter of *The Go-Giver*.)

Two other previous businesses show up here, too. You may have guessed that the incredibly comfortable chair in the Coach's office is custom made at Allen & Augustine, from *The Go-Giver Leader*, referred to here as the "big furniture place . . . down on Dale Drive" that sits next door to Aunt Elle's breakfast kitchen. (And yes, Dale Drive is a nod to Dale Carnegie.) And we couldn't leave this story without paying a brief visit to Iafrate's Café, where so much happened in both previous stories.

The elephant statue that Pindar commissioned for the park in the middle of the city also found its way into this story; as a metaphor of human interaction, that ancient story just seems to get better and better with age.

Aunt Elle herself, of course, is making her second appearance; she was the mentor of *The Go-Giver Leader*. And Pindar, the Chairman who started it all, is once again there in the background. Perhaps one of these days we'll get to see him in person again.

Why is it that Solomon sometimes says "WOOF" and at other times says nothing?

What a great question! In the course of the story, Solomon says "WOOF" exactly five times. As to why he chooses to speak up in those moments and not others, here is a clue: look at the last significant statement that Jackson says (or thinks) just prior to each Solomonic pronouncement.

Can dogs read minds? Do they have the wisdom of ancient kings? You tell us.

ACKNOWLEDGMENTS

No book happens on its own or bursts onto the page from an ivory-towered vacuum. While it may start out in the minds of its authors, it takes the inspiration, ideas, collaboration, and contributions of many to successfully make the journey from drawing board to marketplace—and for us, one of the most enjoyable parts of the entire enterprise is reaching the point where we get to say "Thank you!" on a page like this one.

Our thanks go out:

To our indefatigable and dedicated agents, Margret McBride and Faye Atchison, at the Margret McBride Literary Agency, who were there at the birth of the Go-Giver universe and have been with us ever since.

To the gang at Portfolio, our imprint within Penguin Random House and the best publishing team in the world: Adrian Zackheim the Wise, Will the Weisser (inside joke), Bria Sandford, Leah Trouwborst, Juliann Barbato, Natalie Horbachevsky, Jesse Maeshiro, Tara Gilbride, and Aly Hancock.

To our kind and keenly perceptive circle of early readers and commentators: Jimmy Callaway, Holly Catania, Dan

Clements, Bill Ellis, Christy Ellis, Randy Gage, James Justice, Ana Gabriel Mann, Abbie McClung, Marilyn Mullen, Kathy Tagenel, Bruce Turkel, and Heather Williamson. And to our growing sphere of new readers everywhere—in other words, *to you* for joining us in Pindar's town and helping us to continue exploring Pindar's Paradox: that the more you give, the more you have.

For their specific contributions to this story's DNA, our thanks also go out:

To Dondi Scumaci, for the insight in her fantastic line, "Emotions are important for the journey—but don't let them drive the car!"

To Roy H. Williams (aka "The Wizard"), for his wonderful comment about the story of the blind men and the elephant, in *Magical Worlds of the Wizard of Ads*, which we appropriated and put into Pindar's mouth via Judge Henshaw in chapter 7 ("most efforts at communication are little more than one blind man trying to get another to see the elephant the way he does"); and to the irrepressible George Bernard Shaw and uncannily perceptive author and journalist William H. Whyte, for the hilarious quip about communication ("the problem with communication is the illusion that it has occurred") that Jackson cites in that same chapter. This quote has a disputed origin; it may have begun with an observation by Whyte, then elaborated into its present form by a handful of others, and have nothing at all to do with Shaw. We think Jackson can be forgiven for his mistake, though: it does have a distinct GBS ring to it, and if the erudite Irishman never said it, he certainly could have!

To the magnificent and prolific songwriter Gary Burr, for introducing John to Nashville's Music Row, the heart of that city's entertainment community, which was the inspiration for the Row where the Coach has his little office.

To John's mom, Carolyn, for that great line he heard her say more than once about her experiences as a middle school teacher: "The kids, I understand; it's the adults I have a hard time with," which Jackson paraphrases in chapter 3; and to Kurt Thomas, John's father's conducting teacher, for the lessons on the importance of breathing and naps that the Coach describes in chapter 6.

To The Ritz-Carlton for the elegantly simple line that Rachel has trained all her employees to say: "My pleasure."

To Liberty the cat, Chiquita the Russian Blue, and Ben the dog, for their everlasting companionship and devotion; may we all aspire to be worthy of such unconditional love. To borrow from one of our favorite bumper stickers: "Lord help us to be the people our dogs think we are."

ABOUT THE AUTHORS

BOB BURG is coauthor of the *Wall Street Journal* bestseller *The Go-Giver* and its companion volumes *Go-Givers Sell More* and *The Go-Giver Leader*. A former television personality and top producing salesperson, Bob speaks to corporations, organizations, and at sales and leadership conferences worldwide on topics at the core of the *Go-Giver* books. Addressing audiences ranging from sixty to sixteen thousand, Bob has shared the platform with some of today's top business leaders, broadcast personalities, coaches, athletes, and political leaders, including a former U.S. president. He is also the author of *Adversaries into Allies* and the classic *Endless Referrals*, which has sold more than a quarter of a million copies and is still used today as a training manual in many corporations. He was named by the American Management Association as one of the Top 30 Most Influential Thought Leaders in Business in 2014. A self-described animal fanatic, Bob is a past member of the board of directors of Furry Friends Adoption, Clinic & Ranch in Jupiter, Florida.

JOHN DAVID MANN has been writing about business, leadership, and the laws of success for more than thirty years. As a high school student, he led a group of friends in starting their own successful high school. After establishing himself as a concert cellist and prizewinning composer, he built a multimillion-dollar sales organization of more than a hundred thousand people before turning to writing and publishing. In addition to coauthoring the *Go-Giver* books with Bob Burg, John is also coauthor of the *New York Times* bestsellers *Flash Foresight* (with Daniel Burrus) and *The Red Circle* (with Brandon Webb); the national bestsellers *Among Heroes* (with Brandon Webb) and *Real Leadership* (with John Addison); *Total Focus* (with Brandon Webb); and the culinary coming-of-age parable *The Recipe* (with Chef Charles Carroll). His *Take the Lead* (with Betsy Myers) was named by Tom Peters in the *Washington Post* as the Best Leadership Book of 2011.

Enjoy the entire Go-Giver series!

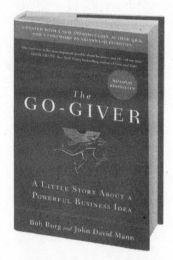

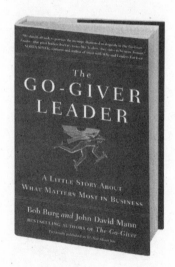

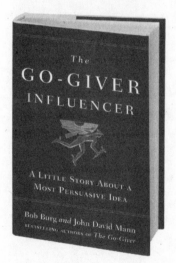

For more information, visit thegogiver.com.

Penguin Random House